# Praise for Jackie
## *Money Vibe*

G000115882

"From the moment I met Jackie, she has been a constant reminder to me what a high vibrating, conscious, kind human being looks like. In her new book *Money Vibe*, Jackie breaks down the true "secret" to creating financial abundance. Implementing the principles Jackie teaches in *Money Vibe*, will put you on the fast track to manifesting all of the abundance you truly desire! If you are wanting to experience a breakthrough in your financial "well-being," then *Money Vibe* is a MUST READ!"

~ **Nicole Zeola**, Co-founder: World of Wellness & WowMoms

"*Money Vibe* is a practical, hands-on guide that offers you a fresh perspective on your relationship with money and success. If you've ever been even a little uncomfortable with either topic, then this book is one investment that you absolutely want to make."

~ **Bruce D Schneider**, Author of *Uncovering the Life of Your Dreams and Energy Leadership*

"*Money Vibe* is an engaging, informed, and systematic catalyst to understand and powerfully transform your relationship with money."

~ **David Kru    r, M.D.**, Author, Business Bestseller *The Secret Language of Money*

"How we think and feel about money has a direct impact our relationship with it, and with the wrong mindset we will always be stressed and struggling about money.

*Money Vibe* helps you create the right mindset so you can have a positive relationship, one that will help your peace of mind and build a profitable future."

~ **Gordon Treadgold**, Inc Top 10 Leadership Expert and Speaker

"Jackie Woodside's *Money Vibe* masterfully weaves stories, facts, inventories, philosophies and practical skills into one inviting and engaging process for readers. This book makes a fascinating read for anyone wanting to improve their relationship to money and quality of life."

~ **Ralph Sanders,** Author of *Break Loose: Anything is Possible and Cyberbullying: Overcome Your Fears and Know that Life is a Choice*

"This profound book provides a comprehensive view on how our beliefs, emotions, attitudes and thoughts impact our relationship with money and what we can do to find true financial freedom!"

~ **Marcia Wieder**, CEO, Dream University[R] and best-selling author

# MONEY VIBE

## YOUR FINANCIAL FREEDOM FORMULA*

*WHETHER YOU HAVE MONEY OR NOT!

# Also by Jackie Woodside

*Calming the Chaos: A Soulful Guide to Managing
Your Energy Rather than Your Time*

*Time for Change: Essential Skills for
Managing the Inevitable*

All of the above are available at your local retailer,
on-line retailers, or may be ordered by visiting:

Money Vibe™ Method:  https://MoneyVibeMethod.com

Jackie Woodside: https://JackieWoodside.com

Conscious Living Media: https://ConsciousLiving.Media

# MONEY VIBE

## YOUR FINANCIAL FREEDOM FORMULA*

*WHETHER YOU HAVE MONEY OR NOT!

## JACKIE WOODSIDE, CPC, LICSW

Conscious Living Media

Tucson, Arizona

USA

# Dedication

Men often dominate the arena of finance and money. Therefore, I decided to dedicate this book to the women in my life who have taught me the most about money, life, having, giving, receiving, growing and living. I am deeply grateful to each of these women for their wisdom and mastery.

The women in my family:

My mother, Norma Hall, for having the strength, courage and grit to raise three children largely on your own, which will always leave me inspired.

My two grandmothers, Grace Woodside and Margaret Tayler, who were "women ahead of their times." Both were deeply devoted to their families and were educated career women in a time when women were not established in the workplace. I can only hope and pray that their legacy and work ethic lives on through me.

My beloved in-laws:

Kay Harker: You teach by example by fulfilling your dreams traveling, birding and taking your grandchildren on wild adventures, while remaining committed to the financial legacy of your mother.

Granny Silvey: Another woman ahead of her time that instilled into her children and grandchildren the love of living simply and happily and who, through her example of prudent spending and wise investing, impacted her family for generations to come.

My mentors and friends:

Colleen Livingston: You have long been a compassionate, loving role model of a career woman who focuses on family, God, and service. I am forever grateful.

Shipley Allinson: Your speaking and teaching gave me the courage to face my fears and live my dreams. I am forever changed from knowing you and learning from your example.

My best friend and spouse:

Heather Harker: I stand in awe of your clarity, heart, vision, faith, belief, and ability to create what you want in life. I am forever grateful to share and co-create this magical life with you.

# Table of Contents

# Before We Begin

On a cold January evening during the final semester of my senior year of college, I strolled into the living room of Byerly House in the small, quaint town of Houghton, New York. Ma Byerly, as she was lovingly called by the students who lived in her home, was reading in the corner of her living room in the glow of a small reading lamp. She welcomed me with an inviting smile and a gesture to join her in the overstuffed chair to her left. I was carrying a handful of bills, two checks that I had signed over to her, and a large plastic Tanqueray gin bottle that served as my coin collector.

"I've got the money for my room," I said. She observed the stash in my hands. "Two paychecks for $325 each, my social security check for $185, $50 in cash and $15 in coins!" I was elated. A few weeks prior, over the holiday break, I seriously wondered if I would be able to finish my last semester. I didn't have the money to pay for my room.

Ma Byerly smiled. It was clear she had had this experience with many students over the years. Her experience left her with the ability to show pride for the accomplishment, concern and empathy for the struggle, and gratitude for receiving the income, all in one fleeting expression.

Four years later when I finished graduate school at Boston College, I was fortunate to be immediately hired by Worcester Youth Guidance Center where I had been working as a social work intern. I didn't take any time off between graduation and starting my job because I had no money left. I had worked full-time during most of my graduate school years but was making very little money. There was a two- or three-week gap between the time I started my job and the day I received my first paycheck. During that time, I literally had no money. My Uncle Tom sent $500 as a gift for completing my degree. I used that to pay rent. When I graduated, grocery stores did not accept credit cards (I know that makes me sound ancient!), but with my Mobil gas card, I could purchase a few things at the Mobil Mart: a loaf of bread, peanut butter, orange juice. It was enough to get by for a couple of weeks.

Most of my life experience regarding money has been living in mere survival. I was born into a lower middle-class family. My mother was widowed when I was two years old, left with three children and a high school education in the 1960s. Despite these challenges, I was blessed to get a great education, thanks to a small inheritance from my grandmother, a host of student loans and lots of hard work.

So, what am I doing writing a book about money and our relationship with it? I am passionate about helping people alleviate the struggle and pain caused not by money, but by our relationship to and perceptions about money.

What I have learned and seen multiple times with my coaching clients and students of my programs is that when we develop higher perspectives and master our thoughts and emotions, our external conditions follow suit. The author Napoleon Hill wrote in his classic book *Think and Grow Rich*: "What the mind can conceive and believe, it can achieve." While that was written in 1937, science today shows that pithy quote to be true and factual. The biggest revolution in human performance today is understanding and applying the concepts of human consciousness, energy, or what I call "vibe." Your Money Vibe lies at the seat of not only how you experience money, but also how you create your financial life.

What will alleviate your stress and anxiety is not only obtaining more money. What will help resolve the strain you experience is changing your Money Vibe. Understanding that statement and implementing it as a way of being is what this book is about. *Your Money Vibe consists of your inner world of beliefs, emotions, attitudes, and thoughts about money.* It constitutes the "resonant energy" that makes acquiring money easy or difficult. Throughout the course of this book, I will teach simple yet profound life-changing strategies that have been used by thousands of my clients and students over the past twenty-five years. You will learn to connect with your inner desires and vision. And perhaps most powerfully, you will learn to change what you believe, how you feel, how and what you think and consequently how you behave which has a direct correlation to the outcomes you create.

The true gift of learning to elevate your Money Vibe is not only will it improve your financial life, but also it will enhance every area of your life. This is true because raising your vibe means you must work on yourself. You must increase your self-awareness, erase limited thinking and beliefs, change negative attitudes, and learn to manage difficult emotions. When you learn to do that about money, you can transfer that learning to every area of your life. Your level of success will rarely exceed your level of self-awareness, personal growth, and emotional maturity because success is something that correlates with the person you become. When you change your vibe, everything changes.

You can learn to dissolve your fears about money, alleviate your stress, and create true financial freedom. The skills and insight you gain from this book will allow you to create the financial experience you desire. However, there is a caveat with that statement: creating true and lasting change requires commitment. That is the enormous difference between the people who continue with life struggles and those who transform the struggles into victories. Those who do the inner work to *change their vibe* and take the necessary actions to *change their circumstances* get results. When you dedicate time, energy, attention and effort toward your financial future you will experience the abundance and success you desire.

Here are some committed actions you can take as you work toward changing your Money Vibe:

1. Become part of the Vibe Tribe. Join me on social media at The Vibe Tribe with Jackie Woodside on Facebook.

2. Post your goal for raising your Money Vibe on the Vibe Tribe page. What is your "compelling why"? Why do you want to do this work of creating financial freedom?

3. Watch the FREE webinar that takes you deeper into the teachings and techniques contained in this book. Go to www.MoneyVibeMethod.com where you can access this free training program. You will find lots of other free resources and fun stuff to support you in elevating your Money Vibe.

4. After you have read the first chapter or so of the book, go to Amazon and leave a review at www.JackiesAmazon.com. Tell others what you are seeing and the possibilities that are opening up for you as you raise your vibe.

5. Go to the Money Vibe website at MoneyVibeMethod.com and download your bonuses: the 52 Affirmations About Money eBook, 40 Ways to Bring More Money into Your Life, The Money Vibe® Method for Debt Reduction, and your own downloadable Money Vibe Model graphic.

# FACTOR ONE: AWARENESS

# You Cannot Change What You Cannot See

# CHAPTER 1

# Money and Its Enormous Impact on Your Life

*Money is the main force of human life*
*at our present stage of civilization.*
*— Jacob Needleman, Author of Money and the Meaning of Life*

If you were to think about money as if it were a person in your life, how would you describe the relationship? Do you get along well? Are you close? Do you argue a lot, or do you get a warm glow of emotion when thinking of it? You have a relationship with money; that is certain. The problem is that the relationship you have may not be healthy and is likely deeply unconscious to you. Your relationship with money is what we will unpack in this book. You can hold money in a positive, proactive, and powerful way. In fact, if you have any hope of true financial freedom, you must.

I have coached thousands of people around pursuing their dreams. What I find stops people are some fundamental fears of lack and scarcity – not having enough and not being enough. When we dig through their fears, they always revolve around ending up with no money, being homeless, destitute and on the streets. Think about it yourself. If you are reading this book, you have a desire for financial success and have dreams you want to pursue. You also likely have dreams that were thwarted at some point along the way. Why did you give up? My guess is that it came down to one of two things: fear of disapproval (often, the unnamed "they" as in, "What will 'they' think or say?") or fear of not being able to make money, losing money or ending up in financial ruin. There is no greater fear for many people than the fear of not having money.

There is such emotional energy around money and yet there is very little support for the cultivation of your inner life – a life of meaning, awareness, development of spiritual capacity, and understanding the self. Our culture is out of balance. There is an intense focus on the outer conditions in our lives and so little attention paid to inner development. Money is central to our existence because in our current culture many of our activities are focused on how to get, make, have, spend, and accumulate it – often without any sense of reason, direction, or purpose other than to make more of it.

Survival instinct and anxiety are encoded in ancient wiring in the brain. We were once hunters and gatherers as a species. We needed to "kill or be killed" to survive. Inside of that fierce landscape and lifestyle was born a somewhat hyperactive nervous system constantly on the lookout for the next catastrophe - the flood with endless rains, droughts that would cause the herds to leave, tigers stalking you as you stalk your prey. Today, many people live in circumstances that they consider stressful and challenging. Overcrowding in cities, traffic patterns, demands of the workplace, and the incessant flow of negative media into our lives exhaust our over-burdened nervous systems. Being faced with constant stimulation may create a feeling of uncertainty and insecurity.

Yet how realistic is this angst and worry? Research published in *The Atlantic* reports that today's young people are the safest generation in history. According to the World Health Organization, more people die from *suicide*, than homicide, wars, and terrorism combined. *Business Insider* notes that the odds of being killed by a refugee terrorist in America are one in 3.6 billion! There is a disproportionate sense of anxiety that does not line up with the actual realities.

Yes, I know that crime, racial discrimination, violence, and terrorism exist. My son is a person of color, so I am sensitive to these harsh realities. However, our neurological stress responses to the concerns we face are disproportionate to the facts regarding our safety.

Genetic evolution occurs very slowly. Our tendency to live in fight-or-flight mode is outdated, yet we largely don't know how to think, feel, or experience life differently.

Our relationship with money is central to this equation. We live in the most prosperous and abundant time in history. People have so much stuff because we have unconsciously tried to mask the underlying fear and angst programmed into our brains by acquiring more and more possessions in an endless search to feel safe and sufficient. We pack on pounds to help us feel secure or numb out the constant undercurrent of uncertainty. Franchises have sprung up to help people deal with their obsessive consumption, hoarding, and the preponderance of "stuff." Instead of worrying about having enough food to survive, millions of people invest billions of dollars each year on weight loss products and programs. The problem is not that we fear for our survival. The problem is that we live in fear of something that is no longer a threat to many people.

What do we do with our overactive nervous systems? Collectively we seem to have geared our evolutionary survival fears toward money. Families divide, marriages end, business partners separate, and friendships dissolve around this dominant element in our society. Our experiences with money are intense because of the way it is linked to our very survival. What is money, anyway? I don't mean that question in the most literal sense. We all know that money is a means of exchange that at some point replaced the barter system. But that does not address the essential power and mystery of money. What does money mean to you? What do you say it is?

The word money comes from the Latin word *monere* meaning to admonish or warn. What is the admonition and warning? Perhaps it is that money has the potential to reveal yourself to yourself and to show you who you really are. Sooner or later, you are faced with hard decisions about how to use your life energy and your money. You must decide what you will do in exchange for money, what you are unwilling to do and for what you will use your money. If you develop the capacity to stop and observe, what you will see if you: your character, values, beliefs, and consciousness revealed right before your eyes.

Whether you realize it or not, money holds all kinds of meaning to you. You have a "money story" made up of the multiple meanings you give to money. I remember sitting with some family friends about ten years ago when two of the siblings were discussing the money they had received from their grandmother over the course of the past decade. Their grandmother, Susan, was a schoolteacher who was wise with her investments. By her later years, she was able to begin gifting $10,000 annually to her children and grandchildren. In my mind, it was a beautiful gift. I'm sure you would think so too. What I heard in front of me was astounding. Susan's grandson was in his mid-20s and was deeply conflicted about the gift he received – a gift that helped him pay for graduate school without accumulating mountains of debt before he even started out in life.

"I didn't even want the money!" he said with stern indignation.

"What?" came my shocked reply, "Why not? Why would you not want to enjoy the love and fruits of your grandmother's life? It is a beautiful gift, and you are so lucky to have this opportunity! Why would you say you didn't want it?"

"Her family-owned slaves in the south," he raged. "That's blood money!" he said, shaking his head in fervent disapproval.

I felt a wave of compassion for the conflict I saw waging within him. He knew that without this money, he would not have been able to attain the educational success he had, at least not without undue financial strain. Deep inside he was a gentle, loving man, with a compassionate heart who did not want to participate in any way toward the harm of others.

"No," I said with my most gentle voice. "It is just money. Anything else that you add on to it from there is what you are determining about the money. You are calling it 'blood money.' I call it a beautiful gift. Which one of us is right? The truth is, neither of us is right because it is just money. What we do with the money that comes into our lives gives us our experience of it. But the money is, and always will be, just money."

His shoulders dropped; his face contorted a bit as if he were trying to fit into a jacket that didn't quite meet his size. He looked up and said, with sad resignation, "Well, that may be true, but I will never have peace knowing that some of that money came off the back of people who had no other choice in how to live." My heart swelled with understanding for him, for me, and for all of us who grapple with our relationship with this powerful means of survival, comfort, sufficiency, and abundance.

And so is our journey with money. What we say about it, how we feel about it, and what we make it mean has an enormous impact on the quality of our lives. Not just our financial lives, but our experience of life itself. Why would I make such a claim? Money infiltrates every area of our mind and lives. You may not think that to be true now, but as we move through this book, you will see the depth at which money affects your future, your self-esteem, your relationships, and your happiness.

Most people think they have little or no control over the impact of money in their lives. They feel that money is external, merely a commodity and, if they are lucky, they will have more coming in than going out. Nothing could be further from the truth. If you do not like the impact money is having in your life, you can change it.

We need to explore whether money is an internal or external phenomenon. At first glance, that may sound like a frivolous inquiry. Of course, money exists outside of our lives. We can touch it, see it and manipulate it; therefore, it is outside of us. While that is true, it is also true that money lives inside of us, in our psyche and our consciousness. To master money, you must master yourself. Why? Because money occurs in numbers and numbers are infinite. When dealing with something that is infinite, how will you ever know the feeling of "enough?"

You can define what is sufficient for you through personal discernment and through money being the servant rather than the master of your life.

In many ways, we are blind to money's impact. We worry about it, wish for it, ignore it, fear it, make decisions based on it, and yet we don't comprehend its role in our lives. Money is a tremendous force in our too-fast, over-burdened, stressed-out lives. It is time we start taking money – and our relationship with it – a little more seriously. We need to understand our current relationship with it and carve out, define, and design the relationship we wish to have with this powerful yet elusive substance. When we do not do so, we end up being powerless to the unconscious allure money has and to the cultural messages we inherit. We need to wake up to our money story, and to our Money Vibe.

# What Can Money Do for You?

Most people have an illusion regarding what they think having more money will do for them. Many people associate money with bringing freedom, relief, less stress, higher status, power, peace of mind and security. They think having money means they won't have to worry and that all their needs will be met. The truth is that money alone will not fulfill all your needs.

I have friends, colleagues and coaching clients who are independently wealthy. They do not need to generate income any longer, having enough money to live several lifetimes without needing to think about money. If you are not in that situation, you might think, "Wow! They're lucky. They don't have to worry about a thing!" The truth is, they worry as much as anyone else. They just worry over different things. You see worry and angst are a state of being.

The *New York Times* recently ran a story by reporter Rachel Sherman in which she interviewed wealthy New Yorkers with assets and income in the top 1-2% of Americans. Sherman found that none of the interview subjects identified as being wealthy or affluent. They preferred to consider themselves "comfortable" and in fact said that "affluence meant never having to worry about money, which many of them, especially those in single-earner families dependent on work in finance, said they did, because earnings fluctuate, and jobs are impermanent."

When you don't recognize that you are experiencing stress, anxiety, frustration, or sadness in and of yourself, not "because of money," you will never know true freedom. You hinge your inner state to external conditions as in, "I'm worried because I don't have enough money."

No matter how much money you have the amount you "need" to feel sufficient keeps growing. It is the ever elusive "enough" that keeps you grasping for "more."

If you had all the money you could ever want, I promise you that you would still experience angst, worry, frustration and all manner of upset – but it would no longer be directed at money. One of my coaching clients addresses her anxiety toward what to do with her time, another toward the fact that he does not have a life partner or mate, and yet another toward his constant fears around health. These people have more than enough money. Angst, worry, fear, and stress are inner conditions that you map onto money! To feel freedom from financial distress, you must give attention to your inner world. All change, all progress begins with self-awareness and growth.

One of my students proved this point to me when she called to let me know she had inherited $1.2 million dollars. While she was grateful for the inflow of money, she was calling because she was worried that it would run out even though she was not spending any of it. She left the money where her family had it invested. She continued to live on her retirement and pension as she had been doing before the inheritance, and what was driving her behavior was fear that the money might not be there.

I asked her if that fear of not having money had been present before acquiring the inheritance. She laughed and affirmed that indeed it had. She realized she had a mental habit of worrying about not having money that did not fit her current circumstances. We then went on to discuss that what needed to change was her fear of lacking money. Otherwise, despite now having financial freedom in the monetary sense, she would never be truly free.

The key, then, is to deal with your inner world while simultaneously creating the conditions for greater flow of money into your life – essentially to master your being and doing regarding money. The good news is that these two go hand in hand. As you increase your awareness and focus on your inner world, you are simultaneously creating the conditions for greater flow of money and all manner of goodness into your outer world. You develop clarity, and confidence, and can move in a way that produces more significant results. Gary Keller and Jay Papasan, authors of *The One Thing*, write "…when you see mastery as a path to go down instead of a destination you arrive at, it starts to feel accessible and attainable. Most assume mastery is a result, but at its core, mastery is a way of thinking, a way of acting and a journey you experience." (*The One Thing: The Surprising Simple Truth Behind Extraordinary Results*). Your job is to master money by mastering yourself.

What we need to grapple with is the fact that money can buy lots of things and experiences. It is an excellent tool in that way. The irony, however, is that money cannot buy what most of us are seeking! Once you get beyond basic survival needs, what most people want are love, connection, happiness, satisfaction, and the feeling of making a difference. Fundamentally, we want to feel that our lives matter. Money can enhance happiness (there are excellent studies to show this), but the one thing money cannot buy is a meaningful life. You and only you can create that.

The problem is that these inner qualities become irrelevant in the face of a mindless, endless pursuit of more money. I have a dear friend who is very wealthy. He has no children and no spouse. He does not travel and has no real hobbies. He doesn't enjoy his work, and yet, when I asked him why he keeps working, he replied, "Well, I have to make money. That's just what you do, isn't it?" I was astounded. I don't share that perspective. To me, making money is not "just what you do." It is only one facet of life. While he is financially wealthy, in my mind, he is not at all free. Is it money you want, or is it freedom? We equate the two when in fact they are not the same thing.

**My definition of financial freedom** is *never having to worry about money, whether you have any or not*! This means not being consumed by thoughts of money, but instead seeing it as a tool of expressing and creating what you want in life. The qualities of financial freedom are peace of mind, generosity, gratitude, joy, and positivity.

People who are financially free see the possibilities for growth everywhere and have more ideas about how to create wealth than they can possibly implement. They are not greedy; rather, they have cultivated a mindset that sees growth, potential and possibility everywhere.

# Money Messages

Let's look at how other people define money and wealth and some of the messages that we receive in our culture. Author and master transformational speaker Tony Robbins says that real wealth is emotional, psychological, and spiritual (*Robbins, Unshakeable: Your Financial Freedom Playbook Creating Peace of Mind in a World of Volatility*). Somehow, I don't believe that is what most people think about concerning money. Money is emotional, psychological, and even spiritual?

Money becomes part of your spiritual expression when you realize that everything in the universe is comprised of energy. One possible way to understand God is as the animating life force energy that creates and sustains the universe. Everything consists of energy: trees, flowers, cars, water, food, roads, and buildings. Everything! Money is energy and so are you. Your thoughts and emotions create the vibratory energy pattern that you put out – your "vibe."

You have a vibe about everything; fitness, relationships, work, life, God, nutrition, places and just about everything else you encounter. This book is about your Money Vibe: the way you hold and relate to money.

Your Money Vibe creates energy that either attracts or repels money. We will get into this notion more as we go along in this book.

For now, it is enough to say that the more you relax and play the game of money and life, the more you create the energetic conditions that supports and enhances the flow of money. It is fun and engaging. What I most love about this "game of money and life" is that money is also concrete. You can count numbers and see the inflow in real and tangible ways.

Warren Buffet, arguably the best investor in the world, once said that the greatest luxury in life is doing what you love. Despite his enormous wealth, well into the billions of dollars, he still lives in the modest house he purchased in 1958 and draws a $100,000 annual salary from his corporation, Berkshire Hathaway. When thinking about money, and your relationship to it, Warren Buffet is the person to emulate. He demonstrates knowledge, wisdom, maturity, and mastery in the domain of money.

Matthew and Terces Engelhart of Café Gratitude are the founders of one of the coolest, most hip restaurants I have ever had the pleasure to visit. In their book *Sacred Commerce*, they wrote, "Money represents the inner quality of abundance, the knowingness of always being provided for." And later they have this creative description of money: Money is a fluid that circulates through the body of humanity.

Think about all of the sayings related to money we have in our culture:

- Money is the root of all evil.
- Money can't buy happiness.
- Money isn't everything.
- It's not about the money.
- Money doesn't matter to me.

Did you notice that not one of these common cultural messages smacks of anything positive? Isn't that fascinating? What does that tell you about the thoughts and beliefs you may have unconsciously inherited about money?

Our paradigms are shifting, though, at least in some segments of our world. When I asked my friends on social media how they define money. Here is a sampling of the answers I received.

- Money is energy.

- Money is NOT outside of God; it, too, is consciousness in form.

- Money is a tool which, when managed properly can help yourself and others.

- Money is love.

- Money is the currency for modern-day sorcery. (That is especially funny!)

The point here is that money carries the meaning that you ascribe to it and the power you give it. You can have little money but be entirely free, happy, and contributing. Or you can have more than enough money and yet experience no freedom.

In 2015, the American Psychological Association found that money was the number one stressor in the lives of Americans. Over 75 percent of parents younger than 50 years old stated that money is a somewhat or very significant source of stress while 25 percent said they experience extreme stress regarding money. These statistics will continue to grow as the divide between the wealthy and the poor continues to grow, and the middle class shrinks.

Technological advances continue to mean a rapidly evolving workforce, which is both exciting and unnerving. We are in what has been dubbed the "YouEconomy." This shift in the workplace means that more people work as independent contractors building a career based on their passions, with greater flexibility, and a vast marketplace. It includes the ability to make money by developing your ideas, doing things you enjoy with skills you have developed — services like Etsy for artists; Upwork for designers, copywriters, and videographers; and Task Rabbit for carpenters, handymen, organizers, and home care workers. Economist Paul Zane Pilzer projects that 50 percent of the workforce will be engaged in the You Economy by 2020. That is a huge shift in how we earn and relate to making money!

What may be more important than money in today's economy are fresh ideas and the ability to execute them. Interestingly, in the early 1900s Charles Fillmore, the co-founder of the Unity church movement said, "Ideas are God's currency." In 2015, author, blogger and radio host James Altucher wrote the same notion in his book The Choose Yourself Guide to Wealth. "Ideas are the currency of life…financial wealth is a side-effect of the 'runners high' of your idea muscle." If you have a great idea and willingness to follow it through, there is a very good chance that you can increase your income by participating in the You Economy. The question remains, however: Will increasing your income alone enhance your quality of life?

The point of examining our cultural messages concerning money and what you say about money is that you have picked up this book for a reason. There is something you want to experience, and you have come to associate that desire with more money. I'm all for that. I've been poor, and I've had sufficient financial means, and believe me, I prefer the latter! But more than anything, I want you to have the fullness of the experience of life that you desire. And I know that simply having more money will not give that to you. I think if you stop for a moment and absorb that sentence, you will know that too.

To have a common understanding, I relate to money as a tool. I prefer to keep things simple, remove any emotional and cultural baggage and just be practical. Money is a tool that can bring experiences and material goods into our lives and the lives of others. It can allow us to support people and causes that we value. It is a mechanism that is central to our civilization. As the quote at the beginning of this chapter indicates, it is the "main force of human life." Given this, we must create a vibrant, healthy relationship with this thing called money.

# CHAPTER 2

# Reality Check:
# Your Financial Fitness

*Awareness is the beginning of all transformation.*
*You cannot change what you cannot see.*
*— Jackie Woodside (Hey, that's me!)*

I teach many self-empowerment courses. I have one on our relationship with time, another on how to design your life, another on how to master your consciousness, and still others on dealing with difficult people and managing your emotions. In other words, I teach a lot of people a lot of stuff about life! I begin every course, every coaching relationship, and every talk I deliver with this: You cannot change what you cannot (or are unwilling to) see. You probably have heard that all change begins with awareness. But what does that mean? In our evolving culture, many words like awareness, empowerment, and meditation get posted in millions of five-step "how to" blog posts, so much so that the depth of the concepts have lost meaning.

Most often when I hear people talk about self-awareness, I hear expressions of what is happening outside of them – as in, "I'm aware that I was furious when he did that!" That is one level of awareness. It is valuable to notice when you are upset. It is important to witness the actions of others around you and know that those actions can, if you allow them to, have an impact on you. A deeper level of awareness, however, is, "What is it about me that has me responding with anger when he does those things?" Self-awareness must always return to the Self! That seems obvious but you will likely catch yourself referencing the things other people do that give rise to your emotions, rather than what it is about you that has you responding a certain way. We will get into this notion more deeply later, but for now, suffice it to say that awareness is critical. *You cannot change what you cannot or are unwilling to see.*

When it comes to money, what awareness do you need to cultivate? We are going to be working on two different domains in this book: the physical plane of possessions, finance, relationships and the like, and the ethereal plane of thought, emotion, beliefs, and attitudes. The goal of this chapter is to initiate deeper realizations about your relationship with money.

Most people repeat a challenging and problematic denial-distress-denial cycle regarding their relationship with money (and any other area in life they find challenging). What I mean by this is that people go unconscious about various areas of their financial life. They simply do not pay attention to their finances beyond the very basics of paying the bills (often late due to the unconsciousness). They do not set financial goals or know their net worth, earning or expenses.  Then, when confronted with a money issue – usually due to an unexpected expense, or the need to do taxes – they experience greater distress, creating a confrontation like one in a rocky relationship where people need to look at the issues they've been avoiding. They need to look to see how far in debt they are now, or how far behind they are on their taxes.

The distress is uncomfortable. People want to avoid it, so when the crisis period is over, the denial phase resumes. You will see similar patterns with addiction. Individuals in the throes of addictive behavior often display tremendous denial about adverse impacts of their behavior until something happens to confront their denial. Often it will be a health challenge, loss of a relationship or job, or loss of financial status that breaks through the denial. This often goes through several cycles before real and lasting change in behavior takes hold.

Our relationship with money and our money behaviors follow this same pattern because psychologically we are addicted to money. By "addicted" I mean doing the same behaviors over and over, despite negative consequences and outcomes, and yet expecting different results.

Without significant outside intervention, many people do not turn their addictive process around. Look at yourself. Do you see where you have behavioral or attitudinal tendencies with money that are unhelpful or even harmful in some way? Do you overspend or ignore increasing levels of debt while telling yourself you will attend to it someday? Do you continue this pattern even though you can see where it is causing you increased stress and lack of self-esteem? These are the patterns to which I refer.

I had a client who was firmly in this cycle for years before hiring me as his coach. Lance was a small business owner who had achieved success in one business before starting another one. His second business was not doing well, and yet he persisted in his efforts.

We began addressing Lance's tendency to spend increasing levels of money on his new venture without reaping financial gain. One day I asked him where the additional funds were coming from, as I was not aware that he had established a credit line and knew that his other business was not generating enough profit to subsidize the spending.

For weeks he assured me that he "had money put away" for the new venture, but there was something in the way he answered that left me uncertain. On one call, I pressed Lance to expound more fully.

"Lance, I know we have talked about this already, but I am concerned about your continued financial losses with no indication of this turning around anytime soon. I have to ask again: Do you have the money to keep pouring funds into this venture?"

He finally acquiesced to the truth. With a heavy sigh he said, "I haven't wanted to tell you this because I know you will make me deal with it. I have been taking money out of the kids' college fund. I've been doing so for about a year and at this point I have totally lost track of how much I borrowed."

"I understand," came my reply. "Your intuition is correct that I will ask you to deal with it. Does your wife know?"

"No. I know she would tell me I can't use those funds."

"Got it. So what are you thinking you need to do?"

"Well, I need to tally up my withdrawals from the account for starters."

On our next call, Lance could barely speak. He fought back the tears as he informed me that he had taken over $90,000 from his children's educational funds. His self-esteem and integrity were wrecked. He had no idea it had added up to that amount of money and felt like a crook.

It was a tremendous turning point for him and to his credit, he used it as positive motivation to get his new business off the ground and making a profit. He told his wife what he had done, and while she was furious, she also appreciated Lance's passion for his new venture. She insisted that he either start making a profit or end the business within the next three months.

With a motivation as deep as an ocean, Lance got to work. It took him nearly two and a half years, but he entirely paid back the funds, including what would have been earned in interest. He joined a 12-step support group called Debtors Anonymous, doubled down his commitment to being coached, and created financial goals and a rigorous spending plan, which he followed explicitly. In essence, he turned his life around when he got out of his cycle of denial–despair–denial. His new business has done so well that he won a regional award for his company. I couldn't be prouder of him and the work that he did to move out of despair and toward the freedom and success we all seek and deserve.

# Awareness and Assessment

To achieve the freedom you desire, you must develop a sense of personal power regarding how you manage and relate to the tool of money. I'm a coach, and coaches love self-assessment inventories. So in these next few pages, you are going to have the opportunity to dig in regarding your current satisfaction and functioning concerning money. These inventories are FOR YOU. The key here is to use them and not just gloss over them like another page in a book.

In fact, to get the maximum benefit from this book, read it and do the exercises in a study group or with a committed partner. You can ask a friend, your spouse or someone at work that you know, enjoy and trust. It doesn't matter whom you choose. **What is important is your commitment to change!** People do not change in a vacuum. We grow and change in relationship with others. That is why coaching programs, therapy, 12-step programs, and other support groups are powerful mediums for creating life-long changes. Give yourself this gift of beginning your path toward financial freedom. Commit to digging deep, doing this work, and building a supportive relationship with a like-minded person to keep your momentum going. Motivation is fleeting. Sustained change requires attention to small changes consistently over time.

I recently read a description of a new program being marketed online. It claimed to take you beyond what other methods of transformation have offered in the past. I was intrigued, so I read further into the details. What I loved about this venture was that they told the truth about how they produce these "better than previously experienced" results. The program required a commitment of 2 hours per day for 17 weeks, plus an additional two to four hours on weekends, and $2000 to get these results! I promise you, if you spend that much time on the principles in this book, you will get results beyond what you have experienced before too, and without putting up $2,000! The point is that profound and lasting change requires more than a fleeting thought or reading a few books. Napoleon Hill called it a "burning desire" in his classic book Think and Grow Rich. Do you have that burning desire for a new relationship with money?

Most of us do not achieve what we want because we get busy with the multiple commitments and demands of daily life. If you want to turn the tide of your experience with money, stop reading this right now. Do not proceed until you get a partner! Put down the book. Grab your phone and call or text someone. (Or maybe you're reading this on your phone! If so, close your e-book app and change functions to your phone!) Call this person your MVP – Money Vibe Partner! Let him or her know that you are excited, committed and determined to create change and you want a partner to be on board with this tremendous opportunity to move into financial freedom as well.

Maybe it feels odd to call someone and ask him or her to go through a money course with you. You have likely internalized the messages that you don't talk about money in polite company. Screw that! This is YOUR life and YOUR financial future. It is time to take money and your relationship with money more seriously.

Ok, I'm done with that rant!

Email me at info@MoneyVibeMethod.com and tell me that you have gotten a partner and who it is. (Yes, that is my email address. It goes directly to me. You will reach me there!). Tell me that you have taken this important step and that you are *committed* to having a breakthrough toward financial freedom!

Below is a simple circle inventory that will allow you to look at various areas of your financial life. Your job is to rate yourself on a 1-10 scale where 1 means you are not at all satisfied with this area of your financial life and 10 means you are fully satisfied. This inventory is designed to be a snapshot of your life as it is today, not how you want it to be in the future. Be honest with yourself. Telling the truth and getting out of denial is the beginning of change. If an item does not apply to you at all, you can mark it 10. For example, if you are retired, have a comfortable income from the investments you have created over the years and you have no prospect of increasing future earning, and you are completely satisfied with that, you would mark that item a 10. Most items will require some assessment score, however. Be careful not to go into denial when you are doing this evaluation. That would look like this: "I don't earn enough to pay the bills, but I am fine with that." If you are not earning enough to pay the bills and you are "fine with that," why would you be reading a book on financial freedom? Be honest. Tell the truth. Let your heart's desires open.

# Financial Satisfaction Inventor

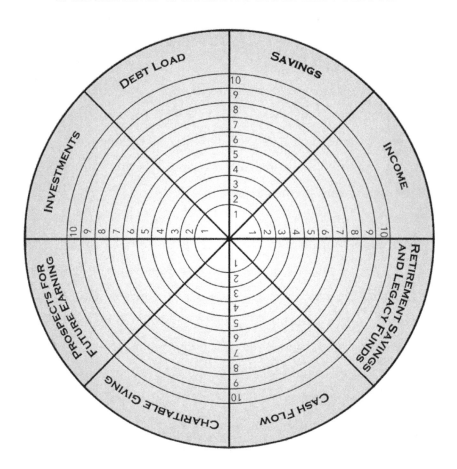

For your clarity, definitions of each category are listed here:

| | |
|---|---|
| **Debt Load** | Your current amount of total debt including consumer debt (credit cards), lifestyle debt (mortgage, car payments, educational loans) and business debt (inventory, mortgage payments, loan payments). |
| **Savings** | Money you have set aside and allotted for a particular purpose e.g., travel, a future large purchase such as a car or home, or unexpected events. This does not include retirement or investment funds. |
| **Income** | Your current financial inflow accrued from all sources (paychecks, alimony, pension funds, trust funds, social security, rental property, any other payments you receive). |
| **Retirement and Legacy Funds** | Money you have specifically earmarked for your post-employment years as well as the money you plan to leave to others. |
| **Cash Flow** | Your monthly and annual financial inflow vs. outflow. If you follow a budget, it could also be your monthly budget. |
| **Charitable Giving** | Money and items you give to organizations, causes and people that you value and support, including tithing and donations. |

| | |
|---|---|
| **Prospects for Future Earning** | Your sense of your ability to earn increasing amounts of money either through work, investments, or inheritance. |
| **Investments** | Money or other assets (real estate, art, business, antiques, collectibles, stock market investments and so on) from which you are expecting to earn money. |

# Going Deeper with Your Financial Satisfaction

This next section is crucial toward improving your scores. The beginning of this process is to gain awareness. But awareness without action is folly. In this next exercise, indicate *what is missing in each area with which you indicated dissatisfaction.* For example, if you rated yourself a "5" regarding your Debt Load, what is it that made you score yourself that way? Perhaps you would write down, "I need to eliminate $15,000 of credit card debt so I can live more comfortably." That is one example of how this inventory works. Look at what is missing in your life that is diminishing your satisfaction.

Self-assessment inventories such as these confront your process of despair–denial–despair. They invite you to look at the realities of how you are functioning regarding money. Allow these inventories to support you and help you move closer toward the experience you want to have with money. Take your time. There is no need to rush through this work. The most important thing is for you to gain insight and take committed action in alignment with the new awareness you develop.

Answer the questions below by writing the concerns, behaviors or circumstances present in your life that informed your rating in each area. Then write what Committed Actions you can take to address these.

**Debt Load:**

_____

_____

_____

**Committed Action(s):**

_____

_____

_____

**Savings:**

_____

_____

_____

**Committed Action(s):**

_____

_____

_____

**Income:**

_____

_____

_____

## Committed Action(s):

_____

_____

_____

## Retirement and Legacy Funds:

_____

_____

_____

## Committed Action(s):

_____

_____

_____

## Cash Flow:

_____

_____

_____

## Committed Action(s):

_____

_____

_____

## Charitable Giving:

_____

_____

_____

**Committed Action(s):**

_____

_____

_____

**Prospects for Future Earning:**

_____

_____

_____

**Committed Action(s):**

_____

_____

_____

**Investments:**

_____

_____

_____

**Committed Action(s):**

_____

_____

_____

Congratulations! By now you should have an MVP (Money Vibe Partner) and have started to break out of your denial about your relationship with the various aspects of your financial fitness. That's a huge first step. Take a moment to appreciate yourself for doing this work and doing it well. Your commitment to change and your willingness to act will pay real dividends!

Your next critical step is to schedule when you will take steps toward increasing at least one area of your financial satisfaction. Place that item in your weekly schedule and tell your MVP what you are going to do and when you are going to do it. If you don't keep a schedule, stop right now, go online, and order my last book *Calming the Chaos*. It deals with the other major source of stress and frustration in our world: Time and managing yourself in relation to time!

Do not move on until you take these actions. Knowledge does not produce change! Knowledge *applied* is what will change your life. You must apply and demonstrate what you are learning to achieve the results you desire.

Congratulate yourself, take a breather, and then let's move on to the next assessment, the Financial Fitness Assessment.

This inventory is designed to look at the structural integrity of your financial life. All creations must be established on a solid foundation of integrity, awareness, knowledge, planning, intention, and action. The items in the inventory below are designed to have you look at various aspects of your financial life with a new eye. As in the last inventory, just tell the truth! Your ascension toward financial freedom begins with awareness. Your current experience reflects your habits and beliefs. We are going to get into those as well, but for now, look, assess, see, be brutally honest, and then take action to improve your current standing.

Your foundation is critical to creating a sense of freedom. Do you see the correlation? You will only bring in money to the degree that you can manage and care for it. When your financial life is out of integrity – as in not structurally sound – you cannot create the conditions conducive to greater inflow.

I had a client years ago that, despite having a successful career as a chef for more than 25 years, always struggled to make ends meet. He had a compulsive gambling habit, mostly in the form of scratch tickets. I saw him win a $25,000 prize and within six months be flat broke, and even in debt again. His son had some legal problems, and he gave most of the money to him, squandering the rest gambling and buying things that had very little meaning to him. I encouraged him to look at his behavior, to see that he was playing with money, largely as a distraction from his discomfort with life. He agreed but continued his patterns.

His next big win was potentially a game changer. He won $125,000 on a scratch ticket. He was initially elated, but soon afterward, within a few weeks, his mood turned sour again. Instead of paying off his mortgage, he bought a new truck that consumed more than half of the money he made. He then purchased a camper trailer in hopes that he and his son would spend time using it together. The camper sat unused for the first summer he owned it, his money was gone, and his son eventually ended up in jail. This is what happens when you don't have a strong foundation with money. He lived his life unconsciously, and that will never create freedom.

On the next page are a series of questions to develop awareness of your current experience, management, and relationship with money. Read this inventory and place a checkmark next to the items that apply to you. Leave blank those that are not now entirely true. To qualify as true, the item must present most of the time. The highest score possible is 25. After you rate yourself, you will see the degree to which you have developed sound financial practices and habits.

| FINANCIAL FITNESS ASSESSMENT | |
|---|:---:|
| I have a regular plan of savings. | ❏ |
| I pay my bills on time. | ❏ |
| My income source/revenue base is stable and predictable. | ❏ |
| I feel sufficient when it comes to money. | ❏ |
| I have returned or made good on any money I borrowed. | ❏ |
| I am current with payments to people or companies to whom I owe money. | ❏ |
| I have 3-6 months' living expenses in an easily accessible account. | ❏ |
| All my tax returns have been filed and all my taxes have been paid. | ❏ |
| I currently live well and within my means, i.e. I earn more than I spend. | ❏ |
| I have excellent personal insurance (life, accident, disability, medical, etc.). | ❏ |
| My assets (car, home, possessions) are well insured. | ❏ |
| I focus on financial growth and have written financial goals for the next year. | ❏ |

## FINANCIAL FITNESS ASSESSMENT

| | |
|---|---|
| Any parking tickets, alimony or child support is paid and current. | ❏ |
| I have no legal issues hanging over my head. | ❏ |
| My will is up-to-date and accurate. | ❏ |
| My debt load and/or investments do not keep me awake at night. | ❏ |
| I know my net worth. | ❏ |
| I have a career that is or will soon be financially and personally rewarding. | ❏ |
| My earnings are commensurate with the effort I put into my career. | ❏ |
| I work with a financial planner or devote time and attention on my own toward my financial future. | ❏ |
| I freely contribute money commensurate with my values and planned giving. | ❏ |
| I do not spend money on things that violate my values and principles. | ❏ |
| I do not fret or worry about money. I am confident about having my needs met. | ❏ |
| I enjoy money and feel worthy of having abundant financial means. | ❏ |
| I have a healthy relationship with money and am comfortable discussing it. | ❏ |
| | |
| **Total Score** | _____ |

As with the Circle of Financial Satisfaction, your job begins when the assessment is complete. While it is not prudent for you to take on multiple goals all at once, because you will likely feel overwhelmed and give up, you will need to create a plan to get your scores up in both areas.

For now, as you continue reading this book, simply choose one or two areas to begin taking action. Some of the items on the Financial Fitness Assessment are easy enough to get done, such as knowing your net worth. There are ample online net worth calculators that can be done in an hour or less. A word of caution: If you have not been paying attention to your financial fitness, your net worth may well be negative (meaning you have more liabilities than assets). If that is the case, don't lose heart. I promise you have what it takes to create a new financial life. You must begin somewhere, and now you know! Seeing the truth and committing to change is the first step. Take heart and continue working through each Factor for Financial Freedom! You are only on the first step! Let's keep going to get you to a better place, and fast!

# FACTOR TWO: YOUR VIBE

## What's a Vibe?

# CHAPTER 3

# What is Money Vibe™?

*The energy of the mind is the essence of life.*
*— Aristotle*

The funny thing about money is that it's not just a monetary commodity. Most of how we function with money relates to our "inner game." Tony Robbins says that the biggest thing keeping people from being wealthy is their brain! I couldn't agree more. To deepen your understanding of and the path toward financial independence, we must explore your psyche, your energy, or what I call your "vibe."

When it comes to the inner game of life, money, and success, there is one crucial factor that has been missing in the ever-developing field of human performance. It is the cutting edge of the human potential movement, and it is time that it started coming to the forefront. You must understand and apply the concepts of this section to change the course of your financial future and your relationship with money. You may develop greater wealth, but you will never have financial freedom without understanding this next section.

What is this crucial factor? It is understanding that everything in existence has a vibratory pattern of energy, or "vibe." The chair in which you are sitting, the house and neighborhood in which you live, your relationship with your best friend and your spouse, your workplace and team, your pet - everything has a vibe because everything is made up of molecules and molecules vibrate. But it is not only physical things that have a vibe. Intangible things have a vibe, too, and these intangibles primarily make up your relationship with money. The intangibles I am referring to are your Beliefs, Emotions, Attitudes, and Thoughts – or BEAT for short. The energetic total of these four items gives rise to your habits, behaviors, relationships, and conversations, which gives rise to your experience of life.

It is your state of consciousness that creates your life. Authors Mark Fisher and Marc Allen, in their book *The Millionaire's Path: Passion, Optimism, and Wealth*, write about this concept saying that everything happening in your life is a mirror image of your consciousness. They go on to say, "Your mind can't grasp this principle if you continue to accept the widespread illusion that external factors determine your life." This is a huge statement. Read that again. You cannot grasp the principle that your life is determined by your consciousness if you continue to harbor the widespread illusion that external factors determine your life! They are calling our dominant belief system an illusion – and I could not agree more.

This reminds me of the life story of one of my coaching clients, Dave. Dave is a man I highly respect and admire. He represents an amazing story of going from nothing to creating a very satisfying, affluent, and fruitful life. Dave did not start out in life with any sense of financial ease. Coming from a modest middle-class upbringing, Dave had a father who was a good man but who liked his liquor a little too much. Early on, Dave decided to make a better life for himself. He started a small carpentry and repairs business while still living in his mother's home. He ran the business from there until he could afford a small, efficiency apartment where he lived well into his 30s. Dave understood the value of money and had a clear notion of where he wanted his life to go. Now, Dave owns two businesses and some real estate. He and his wife live in a beautiful lakefront home in Northern Michigan and enjoy spending summers on their yacht while traveling to extraordinary places throughout each year.

Dave is humble about his success, generous in his giving to his employees, family, and community, and always grateful for what he has accomplished. He is a lifelong learner in every sense of the word – taking classes, being in a long-term coaching relationship with me, working with a personal trainer, changing his diet to improve his health, supporting his employees in receiving coaching and other development work. Dave's story from modest means to financial freedom demonstrates his recognition that his life was not determined by his external circumstances. He may have grown up with some difficulty and not the best role models, but he made a clear determination as to what his life would be and then went out and fulfilled that vision.

There are numerous approaches to having healthier emotions. Many authors write about how to change your thoughts. A hot new topic for people to write about is the study of success habits. Many people write or teach about mindsets. But few of these books, blogs, podcasts, or classes deals with the underlying root of each of these disparate areas, which is your consciousness.

Your consciousness is the total vibratory pattern created by the combination of these four areas. You can change one area but still not have the experience you want. To create financial freedom (or freedom in any dimension of life), you must address the root of your being, which is the vibe you create through your beliefs, emotions, attitudes, and thoughts. We have lived with the false notion that our BEAT creates us – that we are the passive recipient of our thoughts and emotions. Nothing could be further from the truth. When we bring the essential life skill of human awareness to our inner world of experience, we can learn to direct and use our thoughts in a powerful, intentional, and creative fashion. That is the path that I chose, as did countless other people who made the incredibly important decision that their lives would not be determined by their circumstances, but that they could create the circumstances they wanted by changing their inner conditions.

You can feel the vibe of people and places, but you likely disregard this input because you are not yet trained to identify or think regarding vibes. Let's look at it in practical terms first, so you can understand this notion from an experiential standpoint.

You have probably had the experience of meeting someone for the first time at a party or some event and immediately feeling a sense of connection. You like him or her, feel like you could talk for hours, and the conversation just flows. I am not even talking about a romantic charge. Sometimes you meet a new person at a party and instantly "jive." And then, conversely, you may have met someone else at the same party with whom you immediately feel uncomfortable. You don't know what to say and you don't want to hang around them or get to know them. What causes that? Sure, you could say that you and the first person share similar interests, but how can you tell that from the first moment you meet? You can't. That's the whole point. What happens in those situations is that you and the person you like possess "similar energy," whereas you and the person you feel uncomfortable around have very different energy. You might have said, "I didn't like his vibe." You couldn't understand it or put your finger on what it is about him or her that you didn't like. There was nothing tangible. You may have heard the phrase "like attracts like on the energetic plane." That energy is the vibe I am talking about, and it is everywhere.

Vibe goes beyond people, as I'm sure you can now surmise. Think about the last time you walked into a great restaurant and there was something about it that just "clicked" with you. You probably turned to your friends and said, "I like the vibe of this place." Or you left a job interview hoping you would not be faced with an offer because you didn't like the vibe of the office. We use the word all the time without realizing that vibe is a real, yet intangible, part of life that can be used and crafted to our benefit.

Let's keep digging into this. Use your own experiences to help deepen your understanding of how powerful and commonplace vibes are in our lives. Picture yourself walking in the sand on a beach, with the sun on your back. How do you feel when you imagine that? What is the immediate vibe that you get? I've asked hundreds of people this question in workshops over the years, and I almost immediately hear a warm, soothing sigh in the room. Most often people say that the vibe of the beach is relaxing, soothing, expansive, peaceful, and rejuvenating.

Now shift your mind for a moment and imagine yourself walking into Wal-Mart or a Dollar Store. I'm not saying there is anything wrong with these places. My point is for you to get attuned to this notion of vibe. There is a very different vibe walking into Wal-Mart or the Dollar Store as opposed to Saks Fifth Avenue or Nordstrom. This statement is not a judgment of one being better than the other. Different places have different vibes, and when you begin noticing this and how you react to the vibe of various locations, you will be on the path to mastering the most powerful force in the universe, which is energy.

Nikolai Tesla, an American Croatian electrical engineer, and the namesake for the Tesla line of cars, once wrote, "If you want to understand the secrets of the universe, start thinking regarding energy, frequency, and vibration." This is a mind-blowing notion to me. Tesla was an electrical engineer, yet he did not say, "If you want to understand the secrets of electricity." He said, "If you want to understand the secrets of the universe." I don't know about you, but I certainly do. I want to know how life works, how the world unfolds, how evolution occurs. These are all fascinating topics to me, and at our current development in our civilization, money is one of the most powerful "energy sources" in our lives. So, I will alter Tesla's quote to say this: If you want to understand the secrets of MONEY – start thinking regarding energy, frequency, and vibration.

The challenge is the incorrect and disempowering belief that you are the passive recipient of your BEAT – that there is "nothing you can do about it." To start unpacking and debunking your beliefs, you must recognize the root belief that you just "have" your beliefs, thoughts, and emotions. ***You don't just "have them" – you have developed them over your lifetime, mostly unconsciously.*** Most of what causes your distress and difficulty is how you think and what you believe. That may be hard to grapple with but stay open to this idea. You think your thoughts are the truth. They are not! They are just your thoughts. *You must be careful not to believe everything you think!* This is challenging because human beings want to be right about what we think and feel. It gives us solid ground, a place to stand, and a feeling of safety. There is nothing wrong with that except when your thoughts and beliefs are unconscious and disempowering!

To summarize where we are so far, your vibe, or energetic consciousness, is comprised of your BEAT – beliefs, emotions, attitudes, and thoughts. Your BEAT is not set in stone. It can be changed to bring you more experiences that you want and less that you don't. This won't happen in some magical way. Rather when you believe differently, you think differently; when you feel differently, you develop new attitudes. And when you think, feel, and cultivate new beliefs, you will do different things, be interested in different topics and ideas, and be drawn to different people. Changing your vibe changes everything and changing your money vibe will change your financial future.

# CHAPTER 4

# Unlock Your Money Vibe™

*The soul is dyed the color of its thoughts. Think only on those things that are in line with your principles and can bear the full light of day. The content of your character is your choice. Day by day, what you choose, what you think, and what you do is who you become....*
*– Heraclitus*

It is one thing to understand the concept of vibe, but if you do not *implement* the principle to your life, nothing will change. If you don't apply the conceptual knowledge to the way you think, believe, make decisions, and behave, you will not create the changes you desire.

Given that your Money Vibe consists of your BEAT – beliefs, emotions, attitudes, and thoughts — to elevate your Money Vibe, you must "unpack" each of these areas of your inner life. It will require patience, self-awareness and truth telling, but what waits on the other side is financial freedom in the truest sense.

Let's start exploring your Money Vibe with these questions below. Remember, learning the concepts without applying them to your life is simply a form of entertainment. The work here is to begin peeling back the onion of your relationship with money. Be honest. Look at the various ways that you speak about, think about, and use money as you answer these questions:

## 1. BELIEFS:

When you talk with other people about any aspect of money, what is the "tone" of the conversation – upbeat and enthusiastic, worried, and resigned, or some other tone? What do you most often say about money? What beliefs does this reflect?

_____

_____

_____

What do you believe about money? (i.e., It takes money to make money; money is hard to come by; if I had more money, I would be happier and less stressed; and so on).

_____

_____

_____

## 2. EMOTIONS:

How do you most often feel about money? What is the immediate word or phrase that comes to mind?

_____

_____

_____

How do you feel when you pay your bills or make purchasing decisions?

_____

_____

_____

## 3. ATTITUDES:

What attitudes do you have toward people who are wealthy or who have greater financial means than you?

_____

_____

_____

What is your attitude toward work? Is it something that fulfills you or something you wish you did not have to do?

_____

_____

_____

## 4. THOUGHTS

What do you think about as you make purchasing decisions?

_____

_____

_____

What private thoughts do you harbor about money?

_____

_____

_____

As you reflect on these questions, what do you see? Would you talk about your best friend with the same BEAT that you speak of money? Is there an upbeat, enthusiastic vibe to your answers? Or an uncertain, disgruntled vibe? Examine a parallel here. If you went to work every day with the same vibe you described above, would people see you as a positive force in the workplace?

You are not the victim of your BEAT. Your BEAT was created unconsciously. You can consciously create a new BEAT by doing the work in this book, talking with friends about your process, and learning, thereby creating new behaviors and habits and learning to enjoy money.

Below is a Money Vibe Model, which designates the different energy levels in which people operate. This model will help you discern your own Money Vibe. It is a designation of the different levels of vibe that operate in people. The vibe that you create, most often unconsciously, determines your experience in life. Your task is to transform your vibe to higher and higher levels, thus creating increasingly more favorable, pleasant, and harmonious experiences with money and likely life in general. This is because as your vibe elevates, you see the world differently. Your interpretations change, your perceptions are more positive, and you therefore relate differently and make different decisions.

## Money Vibe Model

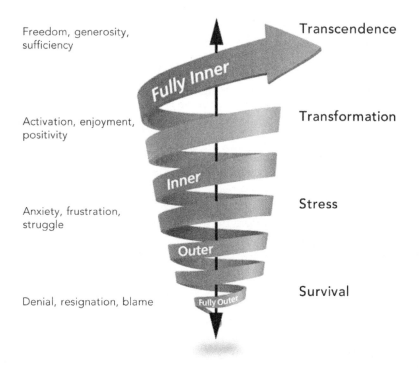

The model is shaped like a spiral or funnel with the lower vibe at the bottom and the higher vibe at the top. The bottom of the spiral is smaller, constrained. The top of the spiral is larger, more expansive. That is important to notice because that is how energy works. Dense, constricted energy is not malleable and therefore difficult to change, whereas lighter, more expansive energy is easier to change. For example, which has a denser molecular structure and energy, a rock or a piece of paper? You can probably see that a rock is denser. Which one is easier to change? Obviously, the paper is easier to change than the rock.

The same applies to your BEAT. When you have very entrenched, negative beliefs, it is harder to be in the flow of energy, ideas, and the higher emotions in life. Like attracts like on the energetic plane. This means that the more negative your BEAT, the harder it is to have a financial ease – in other words, greater flow, greater ease. Suze Orman in her book *The Nine Steps to Financial Freedom: Practical and Spiritual Steps So You Can Stop Worrying* wrote, "It was the attitude with which the client goes into an investment that helps determine whether he or she would make money or lose money." She is pointing to the fact that a person's BEAT impacts not only their inner experience of money but the actual outcomes of their investments as well.

Let's break down each level in more detail:

## Survival: Level One (L1)

People living in the survival vibe have tremendous difficulty emotionally, psychologically, and practically regarding money. There is often poverty or a sense of "just getting by." Even when one has more comfortable financial means, there is an inner feeling of insufficiency, scarcity, worry, and constant struggle with money. The thoughts at this level often are negative or highly avoidant ("I don't want to think about it."). The emotions associated with money are also mostly negative, such as resenting other people who have greater financial success or feeling like there is never "enough." What is missing at this vibe level is the initiative to do more to improve one's financial lot in life. Work is a means to survive. Money flows toward things like buying alcohol, cigarettes and low nutrition foods that appeal to addictive tendencies such as those laden with sugar and carbohydrates (pizza, donuts, pastries) which in turn lead to health challenges that further exacerbate the financial peril. Or the money piles up in the bank and investments, but the internal experience of insufficiency remains. The L1 vibe does not necessarily reflect lower economic means. I have a friend who is retired with a great pension and has enough money to easily meet his monthly expenses. He has a very comfortable lifestyle that includes travel, boats and nice cars. Yet he is constantly worried about not having enough money. One's Money Vibe does not create a direct correlation to one's economic standing.

There is a tendency to blame others or institutions for these problems. L1 energy is unpleasant to be around and very difficult to change. There is little or no awareness that they, themselves, are part of the problem and that their BEAT leads to behavior that repeats the cycle of financial stress, chaos, and crisis.

## Stress: Level Two (L2)

People with this vibe have greater awareness of the role they play in their financial circumstances but are often too stressed, overwhelmed and frightened to try to make substantive changes in their thinking and feelings and, therefore, their behavior. They feel chronic, low-grade anxiety about money that becomes almost entirely unconscious. People with this vibe tend to be hard workers who maintain steady employment, and they relate to work to get ahead. Or they are diligent about their family life, their volunteer role. No matter what they do they have the sense of working hard. Their focus is on changing their circumstances rather than changing their inner landscape, so they continue to repeat emotional and experiential patterns over time. They often are living on the edge financially and emotionally. They have greater hopes and dreams for the future, but because of their lack of inner focus, their goals often result in frustration rather than gratification.

My experience of being a full-time graduate school student while simultaneously working full time and doing an internship is a good example of what L2 looks like - not just by what I was doing, but in my vibe. I was willing to work hard and was focused on getting by and getting ahead, and it was exhausting, frustrating and stressful along the way. I had little enjoyment of the work I was doing. It was all simply to accomplish an end – get through graduate school and be able to improve my financial life. That "in order to" mindset is a hallmark of L2 consciousness.

## Transformation: Level Three (L3)

People with an L3 vibe experience relief of the rat race money wheel. At this level, people tend to have greater self-awareness and spend time engaged in their inner growth and development, recognizing the importance and impact of their BEAT on their outcomes and experiences. L3 people are pleasant to be around. They are confident and often generous with their time and money.

People living at this level have a pervasive sense that everything is ok with them and with life itself. They function well in all circumstances, and their ability to operate with clarity and calm despite even very challenging situations is marked.

They make great team players and friends because they have learned to appreciate the cycle of giving and receiving. They relate to work as a means of contribution and fulfillment. Their financial affairs are often stable. There is a greater understanding of how to make money and how to make money work for them. They recognize money as a powerful tool for creating a better life and therefore feel optimistic and positive toward money and finance.

## Transcendence: Level Four (L4)

At this level, money becomes an important ally in supporting one's contribution and purpose in life. There is an appreciation for the deeper meaning of money in life as it relates to one's identity and purpose. At this level, work is a means of fulfilling one's mission and purpose, another tool for the full expression and enjoyment of life. Money fears and worries are non-existent. There is harmony among one's thoughts, feelings, desires, and earning. Generosity is nearly always present. There is less attachment to material gain.

People living at L4 emanate a sense of personal freedom, joy, and well-being. They experience a profound sense of knowing that they are one with all of life around them. They feel richness in every moment, even within difficult circumstances. They tend to be in awe of life itself.

Do not make the mistake of equating L4 exclusively with wealth. As I have said previously, financial freedom is having a high Money Vibe, whether you have money or not. Some wealthy people never experience L4 with money or any other aspect of life, just as there are people with limited financial means who have a very high Money Vibe.

One of my students, Karen, is someone without a lot of money, yet she has created extraordinary outcomes, including recently buying a new home. Four years ago, Karen was in a severe car accident that left her impaired with a traumatic brain injury. Before her accident, she worked full time as a successful surgical cardiac nurse, ran marathons, was an avid horseback rider, and was enjoying every aspect of her life. The accident and brain injury left her unable to work due to the impact on her cognitive processing and functioning. Her memory was impaired, her ability to focus significantly diminished, and her clarity of thought had all but disappeared. With help from social workers, she applied for and received full disability. Despite the drop in her income level, Karen was determined to get her life back on track. She enrolled in several of my programs, and by consistently applying the principles of those courses (which are contained in this book) she was able to buy the exact home that she wanted in the neighborhood she desired. Her Money Vibe stayed high. She believed she could accomplish her goal and took the necessary steps. Despite limited funds, her Money Vibe was transcendent.

People with an L4 Money Vibe respect money. They are neither reckless with it nor stressed out about it. They honor money for what it can do, appreciate the money they earn and are grateful for what it affords them in life. They do not harbor negative feelings or attitudes about having money or others who have more money.

Conversely, people who have a lower Money Vibe are frustrated and often harbor resentment toward people who have money. I am not talking about overt hostility or disrespect in any way, but in the safety of an intimate conversation, or in the structured setting of the workshops I teach on this topic, nearly every person who struggles financially admits to feeling and thinking this way. They also acknowledge immense frustration with wanting to believe, feel, and think differently about money but feel trapped in old patterns. Most people, however, have their BEAT tied up in negativity regarding money due to our out-of-date evolutionary neurological programming. They have "money issues" that leave them with stress, low self-esteem, worry and a host of negative beliefs about themselves and money.

***It is hard to have a great life when you don't have a great relationship with money.*** That is a bold statement, and I do not mean that it's hard to have a great life when you don't have a lot of money. But I have seen evidence repeatedly that it is hard to have a great experience of life when harboring a negative vibe toward something that is so central to our culture.

All change begins with awareness. On the next page is a grid to help you quickly understand the variations at each vibe level with each segment of your BEAT. Review this chart and look to see where you find yourself in each category.

| Common Characteristics at Each Level of Money Vibe | | | | |
|---|---|---|---|---|
| | **Survival** | **Stress** | **Trans-formation** | **Trans-cendence** |
| **Beliefs** | Money is hard to come by. Work is a means to an end of acquiring money to survive. | Acquiring money takes a lot of effort and work, value of hard work. | There is enough money to go around. I'll always have enough. | Life and money are abundant and to be enjoyed. |

| Common Characteristics at Each Level of Money Vibe | | | |
|---|---|---|---|
| | **Survival** | **Stress** | **Trans-formation** | **Trans-cendence** |
| **Emotions** | Feeling resigned, often blames others for money problems, despair, apathy | Stress, anxiety, frustration, overwhelmed | Excitement about the adventure of earning money and offering service to the world, enjoyment of work | Freedom, joy, gratitude, enthusiasm, expectancy of good |
| **Attitudes** | Negative attitudes toward people who are wealthy or appear to have money. | Uncertain yet determined. Willingness to work hard. | Life is what you make it, including your financial life. | Money is but one tool for doing good and enhancing life experience. |
| **Thoughts** | Thoughts are often crowded with negativity toward people and institutions. Wishful thinking such as winning the lottery or other escapism is often present. | If I work hard enough, maybe I can make things better, but I wish I didn't have to work so hard. Why can't I make it to the next level? | There are ways to be more "in the flow" of money and life and the more I live according to those ways, the more money I enjoy. | Money is a tool I use to do good for myself and others, to contribute and make positive changes in the world. |

# CHAPTER 5

# How to Elevate
# Your Money Vibe™

*When it comes to money, freedom starts to happen*
*when what you do, think, and say are one.*
— *Suze Orman, Author, The 9 Steps to Financial Freedom*

I've spent most of my life worried about money in some form or fashion. When I was in graduate school at Boston College in 1988 and '89, I worked overnight shifts at a community residential home for adults who were Deaf, Blind and developmentally disabled. That meant that I went to school or worked at an internship all day, did course work in the early evening, and went to work from 11 PM to 7 AM five days a week. I would sleep for a couple of hours in the afternoons on days when I had classes, but on internship days, I would often go 24 to 48 hours without sleep.

On top of that insanity, I would scour the Boston newspapers for paid clinical research trials and would sometimes miss classes to be a lab rat for area hospitals. One of the tests involved doing eye-hand coordination tests on one day, then coming back the second day and drinking two large containers that might have contained vodka mixed with orange juice (it did!) in a blind clinical trial to measure the impact of consuming alcohol on my precision with the drills. Lucky for me they paid for a cab to get me to and from the trials that day!

My professors and friends thought I was crazy for the things I did. All I knew was that I needed to survive. "There has to be a way for me to get by financially, and I will find it" was my constant vibe. I was nothing if not resilient. But you can see from this description that I was living in a stress vibe regarding money. "If I work hard enough, I can figure this out." And work hard, I did.

In 1995, I wrote in my journal, "I spend time reading and studying about prosperity, but I am not advancing toward a more prosperous life – no new clients, no raise at work, no house purchase. I am doing this prosperity work, but I am doing it from a scarcity mentality! I am always worried there won't be enough money now and in the future. I need to retrain my thinking and take on a new vibe. The universe is an abundant place. There is more than enough money to go around. I can spend money on others and myself without the fear of running out. The Universe has always provided me with what I needed. I won't go without the things I need. I need to realize that money comes to me and affirm that truth until it is a fact and belief in my life." I was wracked with fear about money my whole life until I realized that changing my outer circumstances by working harder was not going to change my overall experience of money and sufficiency.

So how did I get from that experience of constant struggle to just get by to the way my life is today? Mastering the concepts in this next section of the book is perhaps the most important skill set you will ever acquire. Many people don't accept these principles because they are simple. The trick is that while the principles are simple, their mastery is not. It takes constant self-observation, humility, attention, willing-ness, focus, and practice. But applying those attributes to these principles consistently over time leads to an entirely different experience of and with money.

Clients and friends frustrated with their experience of money who have heard my story repeatedly ask me how I changed my financial life and how they can do better. They want to know how they can earn more and feel less stressed about money. When I tell them the strategy I used, they seek something more complex and don't want to believe doing inner work can change their experience of money and life. There is a formula, and it's not at all complex, but you must be willing to do the inner work of creating change.

# Your Human iOS*
# (*Internal Operating System)

To change your Money Vibe, we need to go a little deeper into the principle of how it got set up in the first place. You now understand that you are not a passive recipient of your Money Vibe. You created it unconsciously through absorbing the messages and beliefs in our culture, which became the lens through which you have interpreted your life events.

I have spent thousands of hours over the course of my career talking with people about the difficulties in their lives. What I see repeatedly is that people want to feel better, but they don't realize that if they keep thinking the same thoughts and talking about the same emotional difficulties, they will keep having the same experience in life even though the cast of characters and setting may change. They have habitually come to see the source of their angst or upset or despair as outside of them – as if they are having difficulty because of their job, friends, finances and so on.

It requires strength of character and emotional maturity to recognize that the source of any emotion or state is within. The brain is conditioned to look outside for the source of our problems as a mechanism of survival. The most powerful thing you can do for yourself, and your financial future is to realize that all inner states and conditions, which create your vibe, depend on you. Understanding this concept is crucial because results arise from actions and actions arise from states.

In 12-Step programs such as Alcoholics Anonymous, there is a slogan: "If you keep doing what you have been doing, you will keep getting what you have been getting." That is not only true of our actions but our thoughts and emotions as well. If you keep thinking and feeling the way you have been thinking and feeling, you will keep getting what you have been getting. In fact, I believe that changing your thinking and feeling must precede changing what you do.

To change your inner experience of money or anything else, you must first believe that it is possible to do so. Take a minute right now. Stop and ask yourself that question: Do you think that you can change your experience of money? Do you believe that you can have more money? A lot more? Do you believe you can be wealthy? If not, why not? What does being wealthy mean to you? We are going to get much deeper into financial beliefs and how they impact your experience of money in the next chapter. But for now, you must address whether you have become resigned about your financial future. You are reading this book, so you have some hope. But on top of hope, you must add awareness, willingness, and consistent practice. That is the key to creating change.

To create consistent change in your financial life (or any other part of life for that matter), you need to understand the basic formula for how human beings operate. There is a somewhat mechanistic structure to human beings. It looks something like this:

There is part of our personality structure that is called the ego. The function and role of the ego is two-fold.

First, it supports your executive functioning in the world so that you can get things done. You go to work or school, take care of your home, and pay your bills, and so on. In the Freudian understanding of the ego, it is the psychological apparatus that mitigates the tension between your impulses and your values and societal expectations. So, in that sense, the ego is a good thing. You want to be able to weigh the pros and cons of storming out of a business meeting because you can't stand the office politics any longer!

But the other function of the ego is the one that we need to grapple with in this book. It is this second aspect that causes difficulty for people who are growth-oriented and want to create change. That function is that the ego is designed to keep us safe from anything that feels threatening – and the ego is at risk by nearly anything unknown, new, and beyond the comfort of the familiar. The ego isn't designed for happiness, but for safety. Your brain is running on old software that needs updating.

Let me give you an example. When I was a social worker serving abused children in multi-stressed families, it baffled me when young children were placed in safe, loving, caring and attentive foster home settings and yet almost 100 percent of them wanted to return home. I am not talking about parents who are "a little unfit." I am talking about the worst possible home situations – where there was often no food, no adult supervision, drug use occurring in front of the children, physical and sexual abuse, and many forms of violence. Still, when asked, the children would want to go home.

We feel comfortable and safe when we are surrounded by what is *familiar*. People have varying degrees of skill and flexibility when dealing with change and new circumstances. So, changing your Money Vibe may not be as easy as it seems. I wrote about that in my first book *Time for a Change: Essential Skills for Managing the Inevitable*. I explored the notion of personal change temperaments, meaning how adaptable and open you are when facing change. For people who have a sensitive change temperament or who are what I call "change averse," the ego sees something unfamiliar and signals: WARNING! DANGER AHEAD!

Neuroscientists Andrew Newberg and Mark Robert Waldman, in their book *How God Changes Your Brain*, discuss this phenomenon from the perspective of brain function. They write that our difficulty changing our Money Vibe results from this: "After spending decades building a somewhat stable personality to handle life's tribulations, the brain is hesitant to alter its underlying beliefs. After all, even if your behavior is dysfunctional, it has helped you to survive, which is what your brain is primarily designed to do. It took decades for your brain to form these habits, and it's not easy to turn them off. Old neural circuits do not disappear, especially if they are tinged with negative or stressful memories."

I recently hired a strategist to help me re-engineer some aspects of my business. It was astounding to me to see how differently he and I think about business. The guy is brilliant. But time and time again I found myself saying, "That makes perfect sense. I wish I were more inclined to think that way, but I can only think the way I think." That is a true statement and one that applies profoundly to your relationship with money. You can only think the way you think unless and until you have significant exposure to new and different ways of thinking about money, which in turn causes you to re-evaluate your Money Vibe. Working with this strategist exposes me to new ways of thinking, which I can then incorporate into my BEAT, which in turn raises my vibe.

I was teaching a Money Vibe class recently, and in the first week of class I asked the students to describe how they feel when they think or talk about money – what is their vibe? The answers were that they predominantly feel stressed, anxious, weary, tired, constrained, and disempowered. Then I asked them if they felt that energy would help them create a greater inflow of money in their lives. They all laughed! Of course, people who are negative about something don't tend to bring a lot more of it into being. If people are negative at their job, they often don't get promoted. If people have a negative vibe about dating, they often remain single. Negativity is a "repellant vibe" that blocks the good things you desire!

The energy I associate with financial freedom is enthusiasm, excitement, and expectancy! You may not realize it, but right now you have the power to create a new direction in life and your financial future. You have been determining your direction all along, but instead of creating what you want, you have likely been unconsciously conjuring up stories of unworthiness, stress, and strife. Living with a vibe of enthusiasm, excitement, and expectancy changes everything. When did you last feel genuinely enthused about your life, excited about what is happening and expectant about a more positive future? I call this the Four Es of Financial Freedom: The Energy of Enthusiasm, Excitement, and Expectancy!

It is not the way most people feel about money! Too often, you get swept up in a sea of negativity and do not even realize it! I hope you will join me in my passionate mission to change the vibe on our planet!

You are the cause of your financial life. Never waiver from that belief. Always claim that you are solely responsible for your life. You will find life much easier to navigate that way. Jacob Needleman writes, "The mind has to become convinced that the only source of its well-being is consciousness." (*Money and the Meaning of Life*).

With that, let's go deeper and work this through with another example. A young girl wants to go to the movies with her sister. She approaches their mother with the request. Her mother looks frazzled and somewhat annoyed. "You know we don't have extra money for foolish things like that. You should know better than to ask." This situation probably happens in millions of households every day. But what happens internally to the child is where we need to focus our attention. The child says, "I need to stop asking mom for things. It's not okay to ask. It's not okay to do things that I enjoy. I need to learn to work so I can have money and help my mom."

She then starts bringing those interpretations to other situations where money is involved. Her grandmother takes her out for an afternoon and offers to take her for ice cream. The girl declines. She doesn't know why she refuses, but somewhere in the back of her mind is the notion that she should know better than to ask for or expect frivolous things. Then the girl is a young woman. She wants to go for a get-away weekend with some friends but decides to stay back at college to work a couple of extra shifts at her campus job to bring in more money. She doesn't say the words, but somehow, she knows that going away for the weekend is frivolous and staying back to bring in extra money will equate to her feeling of self-worth.

She lands a job right out of college, and all her new friends at the office are the "hard-working crew." They are the ones arriving early, staying late, and not minding putting in the extra hours on weekends. This behavior becomes her norm, and she barely realizes that other members of the office play in a kickball league after work once a week, went on a weekend kayaking excursion last month and go out on Thursday nights for drinks.

Eventually, she gets married and has a daughter of her own. One day, when her daughter is old enough to enjoy doing things with friends, she asks her mom if she can go out for a movie.

I'll bet you can finish that story, can't you?

To summarize this process of the Human iOS so that you can apply it toward money and everything else in your life:

1.  Something happens that is as routine and random as the weather.

2.  You make it mean something about yourself or the world.

3.  You unconsciously carry that interpretation to other situations.

4.  That unconscious interpretation becomes your belief system.

5.  You surround yourself with others who think, believe, and behave the same way thereby reinforcing your beliefs, behaviors and world view.

6.  You think, "That's just the way life is."

No, it's not just the way life is. It is the way you have become.

The ego has a mechanistic stimulus/response pattern to it. What that means is that once your Human iOS is set, and your BEAT is in place, you develop a very predictable pattern of how you experience and respond to life. That predictable pattern establishes the vibe that both creates and attracts what happens in your life.

I had a coaching client a few years back who inherited $250,000 when her parents both passed away. My client, Sarah, is a very upbeat, optimistic, "high vibe" person who thoroughly enjoys life. While she is not wealthy, she runs a successful small business and enjoys the fruits of her labor. When Sarah learned about the inheritance, she was elated and talked effusively about how grateful she was that her parents had shown such care for her and her sister Maureen in putting this money aside for them to enjoy. Maureen has a different BEAT and vibe. She has always struggled financially, living on public assistance in a tiny, run-down trailer home. Upon hearing the news of the inheritance they would soon acquire, her response was markedly different than Sarah's and yet completely in alignment with her vibe. Maureen responded with frustration and anger, wondering why her parents waited so long to give them the money. She lamented about how she would not give any of the money to a financial services broker as "they are all crooked thieves" who would take her money, and she made no mention of how the inheritance would help improve her living conditions. Her entire perceptual frame, one of difficulty and struggle, continued to perpetuate her experience of money, despite the fact that she just inherited a quarter of a million dollars!

This story is a perfect example of how the Human iOS operates. We unconsciously transmute our interpretations and perceptions into our belief system, which gives rise to our emotions, attitudes, and thoughts, which translates into our experience of life. We also unconsciously gravitate toward people who think and believe similarly which then reinforces the beliefs we have established.

To what thoughts are you giving power? With what feelings do you identify? Most people do not realize the extent of their inner feelings and thoughts of scarcity (There is not enough), worry (There will not be enough) and personal insufficiency (I am not enough). These are all lies that the ego creates to keep you from taking risks or venturing too far from your comfort zone.

Living with a high money vibe is a beautiful way to live, especially given how central money is in our culture. What is money for anyway? That is an interesting question. What is your answer? What purpose have you ascribed to money? I believe that money has three roles in our lives:

1.  To increase, elevate and expand what we can do, have and experience.

2.  To increase what we can contribute and create.

3.  To impact the greater good of our families, communities and the world.

Having a strong Money Vibe increases your ability to achieve all of these three elements. It also will serve toward the elevation of your self-esteem (when you align your money with your values) and having a higher self-esteem increases your money vibe. It is a positive feedback loop that continues to elevate and expand. People who believe in themselves and have a high consciousness create great things. The higher your vibe, the less inclined you are to let external circumstances dictate you. You are more focused, more confident and more at ease. The more your vibe increases, the more you believe that you can accomplish greatness. And our world needs people who envision, act on and create great things.

# What is Financial Freedom?

I am happy to tell you that there is a way out of this habitual and programmed way of operating. The only way to truly have financial freedom is to create a new money vibe. By now you must have a good sense of your money vibe and the level at which you are operating. If you are still uncertain, your reactions to your circumstances will be a clear indication.

One of my Money Vibe students recently posted online that she must have some unexpected income coming her way. Puzzled as to what new opportunity she received, I read on. "Because my mechanic just told me that I need new struts and an alternator for my car that will cost me over $2000, so I must have money coming my way soon!" That is financial freedom! Never having to worry about money, having faith that there are sufficient means for the ends and trusting that Life will provide, and her needs will be met.

The first place to begin is to recognize that your current BEAT is based in your past: your experience of life up to this point. That is the first problem. You will not create a new experience from an old paradigm. That is why it is important to spend time with people who reflect the future self you are creating rather than the "you" of the past.

Science is showing more and more that we create our perceptions through the interpretation of the electrical impulses received by the brain. Cognitive neuroscientist Anil Seth, in his April 2017 TED talk, stated it this way: "Perception has to be a process of informed guess-work in which the brain combines sensory signals with its prior expectations or beliefs about the way the world is to form its best guess of what caused those signals. The brain doesn't hear sound or see light. What we perceive is its best guess of what's out there in the world."

In other words, we create meaning from our perceptions, but our perceptions are informed by "prior expectations or beliefs about the way the world is." This notion is an important piece of information, and it is crucial to changing your money vibe. If your beliefs about money exist in the lower vibe levels (as is the case with many, if not most, people), you will translate your outer world through this constricted lens.

To change your vibe, you must change where you "locate your identity." What I mean is that you must shift from having your percep-tions derived from *your* past to having your perceptions and sense of self based on *your desired vision and what is possible*. The way you know yourself, whether you realize it or not, comes from the accumula-tion of experiences you have had up to now.

To have a different financial future, you must first change the way you interact with your thoughts and emotions. The Dalai Lama posed an interesting question that bears consideration here: Can the mind change the brain? This begs the question: Are the mind and the brain different entities? I believe they are. Understanding that distinction and utilizing the incredible power of your mind to direct your brain is a key element of elevating your Money Vibe.

Your mind is the life source that animates your being. It is connected to the eternal source of all creation. It has enormous intelligence and profound creative capacities when we understand how to use and direct it. Your brain is the organ of miraculously complex neurological systems that is the seat of your experience of life. Training your mind to maximize the astounding potential of your brain is extraordinarily exciting and enthralling. It is a lifelong passion and pursuit of mine.

# Catch It, Challenge It, Change It

Rather than being an unconscious participant in your inner dialogue, holding onto it as Gospel Truth, you can begin focusing your mind and using it in ways that you direct and orchestrate. You become the master of your thinking. This shift occurs through a three-step process I call "Catch It, Challenge It, Change It."

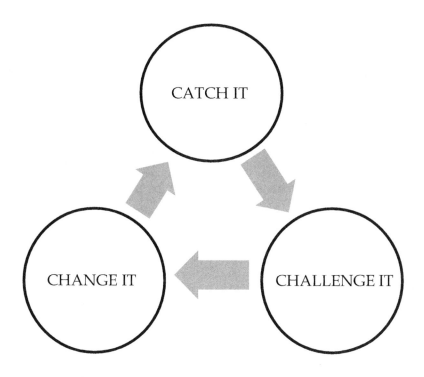

**CATCH IT:** Beginning with neutral, impartial self-observation, start to notice the inner dialogue you have about money. Watch what you say in your conversations and how you feel when you experience an unexpected expense or even a sudden inflow of money. Like my student who received over a million dollars of unexpected income or my client's sister who received a quarter of a million dollars inheritance, their response demonstrated fear and angst.

These are the ways you begin noticing your money vibe. How do you respond? What do you say? What do you think? Notice your inner world and become aware. Tell the truth if only to yourself. Know that the vibratory pattern of your BEAT causes your discomfort and suffering.

Don't pretend that your financial problems are beyond your control. Once you believe you are at cause in your life and never depart from that position, you will find that your financial future improves dramatically. Waiting for things outside of you to change gives away your power and authority. Believing that you alone are the creator of your life is the most empowered position you can employ.

You begin this process of self-empowerment by becoming keenly aware of what you are thinking, feeling, and saying. You may believe you are responsible for what you do and not for what you think. *A Course in Miracles* teaches that you must become fully responsible for what you think because it is at the level of thinking that all action and behavior begin.

You identify your BEAT simply by noticing – through impartial self-observation. Then, when you observe thinking, conversations and behaviors that are not what you want to create and experience, you go to the second step.

**CHALLENGE IT:** Challenge and disempower thoughts that do not reflect the experience you want to have by "talking back to the thought" and debunking it. That may sound like a ridiculous notion. Am I suggesting you walk around talking to yourself? I suppose I am. When it comes to changing your inner landscape, you must begin asserting the authority of your higher vibe mind over your unconscious, habitual thought patterns. You train your thinking and create a new vibe. Use your mind to train your brain.

Here is an example of how this works: Suppose there is a part of your work that you don't enjoy; maybe paperwork or a particular meeting. As you approach that task you might think, "This is such a drag." As you notice that thought (Catch It), you can debunk it (Challenge It) by asking, "Is that what you want to experience? What else could you think and feel about this? How could you make a difference for others and yourself?" As you do this you are asserting authority with your higher vibe mind over the lower vibe, habitual thoughts that often drag you down. You are choosing a different thought which generates a different feeling, which raises your vibe.

Simply by recognizing that you have this ability is the first step. Your brain is a system of habitual responses. *How you alter those habitual responses is by focusing not on your immediate unfiltered reactions to life, but on what you want and desire.* Author Mitch Horowitz in his book *The Miracle of Your Definite Chief Aim* writes about psychiatrist Jeffrey M. Schwartz, who developed a program to help people overcome obsessive thoughts. In this program, patients are taught to redirect unhealthy, worrisome, obsessive thoughts toward something that is healthy, pleasant, and desirable, such as great music, food, laughter, nature, and so on. Horowitz summarizes, "You are not built to control your mind through an act of will alone. Trying to control your thoughts or emotions is often frustratingly evasive and depleting. But you are built to gravitate toward passionately felt desires… This directed mental force eventually results in rewiring the brain's neural pathways, through which electrical impulses travel." You change your habitual perceptions not by unconsciously following the conventional interpretations your brain has developed, but by altering them by focusing on your desires, passions, and higher mind.

You disempower lower vibe thoughts by challenging your BEAT from the perspective of your higher mind. Here are some questions geared toward disempowering the lower vibe mind:

- What do you want to experience?

- Do you want to continue believing that?

- What has that thought created in your financial life?

- Where does that thinking lead?

- What higher emotion could I choose?

I tend to ask myself these questions with a not-so-minimal twinge of sarcasm. It would sound something more like this: "Is THAT what you want to experience?! (As in, "You can do way better than that!"). As your mind grapples with these confronting questions, it begins to change. Of course, you don't want to continue creating emotional turmoil over money! No one wants that experience – and yet 90 percent of Americans say finances create emotional stress for them.

**CHANGE IT:** How you then change your mind is by replacing the lower vibe thinking with what you want to experience. Instead of, "Look at those folks. They are so lucky to have that gorgeous house. I'll never have that," you identify the lower vibe thought and then ask, "Is THAT what you want to believe? If you continue thinking that, how are you ever going to grow your finances? Is that objectively true that you'll never have that? No, it's only true if you believe it and then act that way."

Then you transform the dialogue. "Good for that family. I can see myself in that kind of home. That house fits my vibe now and even more so as I grow and prosper." This approach is not "Fake it 'til you make it." It is transforming your mind through self-awareness and training.

Let yourself feel the lower energy thought, and it will pass through you. When you acknowledge your negative thoughts and feelings without attaching to them (and that is the trick), you can feel them, let them pass through you, and then transform them.

Replace lower aspects of your BEAT with what you want to experience. You can come up with a few practiced visions that you repeat and enjoy. One of my visions is my family spending time at our summer cottage, sitting on the deck overlooking the St. Lawrence River just before sunset, feeling relaxed and happy. I use that image to reset my state.

I also have mental visions of giving my spouse a high-five after accomplishing a big goal. I carry an emotional imprint of how these images feel and they immediately shift me into a higher state. I have taught this method repeatedly and have watched hundreds of clients and students change their inner landscape and their financial lives.

Remember I said that these principles are simple, but not easy to practice? Most people try this once and think that their habitual lower vibe thoughts won't return. They will say to me, "Oh, I tried that. It didn't work."

I always ask, "Really? You mean you were not able to transform the thought or feeling with that three-step process?"

"Oh, no, it did transform, but the next day it was back just like before."

No kidding! Of course, it was back! I can imagine it was back not just the next day, but also the next hour, or even the next MINUTE! That is what I mean when I say this process is straightforward and simple, but not easy.

It has taken your brain decades to create the neuropathways you have established, and they won't just transform overnight. The process of changing your thinking is exhausting. It takes energy to think in new ways.

Your thoughts are embedded in your brain through neural networks. Think of neural pathways as a trail in the woods. Taking the same route repeatedly creates a clear and easy route to an intended destination. As the trail wears over time, it becomes less cumbersome to walk that way. Veering off the path requires effort, as you must clear away the forest growth to get to the same destination. The same applies to your brain, which gets patterned with consistency and repetition. Your thoughts and responses to life are habitual, whether you recognize it or not. It takes concerted focus, effort, support, and practice to unwire and rewire your brain to think from a higher perspective.

Bring rigorous self-examination and willingness to change the thoughts and feelings repeatedly as they arise. You can change your BEAT through practicing the principles in this book. Science is teaching us so much about how to enhance our life experience by using our brain and, in fact, training our brain in new and different ways. Neuroplasticity is the brain's amazing capacity to change and adapt as the result of how we choose to interact with our internal and external environment. With the advent of this discovery and understanding that the brain can and does adapt to our environment, it now becomes scientifically verified that you can change your BEAT. Your brain will acclimate according to your focus.

Pay attention to the level of your thinking about money throughout your day. Notice how you respond to the day-to-day events. Observe the quality of your conversations. Are you taking responsibility or speaking as if you have no control? As you practice rigorous, non-judgmental self-examination you will notice the perceptual level from which you live and experience life.

I am writing this section of the book while living in my 1950s summer cottage in Upstate New York. While I love it here, owning an older structure that sits empty for nine months out of the year brings many surprises along the way.

In one day, I had interactions with a man who is replacing my broken sewer pump, another who came to fix my boat, three Amish men who are replacing my shed roof, and the man who is repairing my dock! In each conversation, I was mindful of the energy I was creating. You can imagine how much money is flowing into each of these repairs, and yet, through this artful practice of creating my vibe, each conversation was pleasant, each contractor gave me very affordable prices, and the work is all getting done with ease.

Neuroscientist Andrew Newberg, M.D. writes, "So what do you do when all of the subtle, and not so subtle, self-doubts kick in? You can do several things: suppress them, evaluate them or ruminate on them. Neurologically it's actually easier to suppress them, because the more you keep your mind focused on your optimistic belief of success, the more you will inhibit the functioning of your limbic system, which generates doubt and fear." (*How God Changes Your Brain: Breakthrough Findings from Leading Neuroscientists*). To suppress the thoughts does not infer to pretend that the thought is not there. This is a key distinction in understanding how to elevate your vibe. You do not feign happiness when you are sad or act joyful when you are angry.

That is inauthentic. How you suppress your lower vibe states is by simply *acknowledging them*. If you allow yourself to feel a state but not identify with it as being whom you are, or being the truth of your life, the state will pass and you can choose a higher thought, a more powerful state.

Your goal is to go just *one step higher* in consciousness from where you are now. If you find yourself in constant survival thinking, your first task is to recognize that is where you are operating, and then change your thinking just to the next highest level. Most often that means beginning to understand that with effort and focus you can make a difference in your financial life. You give up on your cynicism, blame, and despair and get actively engaged in creating different thinking, looking for new and different opportunities and engaging in higher level conversations.

Massive overnight transformations in consciousness happen, but they are rare. Most people plod along, changing their inner landscape a little at a time. Knowing you "should" do certain things or be a certain way does not make it happen. It is not enough to know important principles; you must demonstrate the principles you know in every aspect of your BEAT. There is no limitation on how you can experience life with the vibe you create.

To practice this three-step process, you must possess one prerequisite belief. You must come to recognize that your thoughts are not "the truth." Your thoughts are just what you think. They are neurological firings in your brain. Many cultural and evolutionary factors program your BEAT. You believe you are a "free thinker", but nothing could be further from the truth. Your thinking primarily depends on the vibe you experience and create. The people you are around, the messages you hear, and the culture all impact how you think, how you act and what you believe.

If you spend time with positive, proactive, and productive people who are committed to success, it will impact your "success vibe." If you spend most of your time with people who chronically complain and who have a low vibe toward life, money, and success, it will drag you down.

Social influence makes us gravitate toward the characteristics of those around us, including their beliefs, opinions, and attitudes. That is why we pervasively see "red and blue" states across the U.S. People with similar political and cultural values tend to gravitate toward one another. There are even geographic locations that are considered "liberal enclaves in conservative regions" such as Austin, Texas, and Asheville, North Carolina. You cannot underestimate the impact of the vibe around you and how it influences your thinking, beliefs and therefore the outcomes that you produce.

I once worked for state government where there was a powerful vibe about work that reflected people's feelings that they "had to work" and had "no freedom" about coming to work. The cultural vibe in the workplace was stifling. I believe that freedom is something you give to yourself, not something granted to you by an outside entity, so it was an awkward "fit" between the workplace culture and my BEAT and my vibe.

I stayed in that job about four years. During that time, I worked a flex schedule (unheard of in those days of state government), was paid the salary I asked for even though it was beyond the standard pay grade for the position I occupied and challenged the status quo regarding our service delivery models. I determined my freedom through clarity, my BEAT, and my larger purpose. I believed I was free to test, make requests, speak my mind, choose my thoughts and feelings, and act within the framework of the system. None of these things made me popular among my peers, but I was clear on how I was going to mold my career and my experience.

Freedom, including financial freedom, comes from your BEAT. There is an opportunity for freedom in everything you do. Viktor Frankl made this notion famous in his classic book *Man's Search for Meaning* in which he declared that the last of human freedoms is to choose one's attitude (BEAT) in any given set of circumstances, to choose one's way.

You will know that you have changed when you have a different reaction to familiar stimuli. Observe your reactions to your financial affairs. Changing your BEAT changes your reactions. I'm not talking about being a little happier. A little alteration in your emotions is not transformation or a change in consciousness. When your vibe is consistent over time and a myriad of different circumstances, you will have achieved inner change. To change at this deep level, you must desire something so different from what you now know that you are willing to commit yourself deeply to a new way of thinking and being. There is no problem whatsoever that cannot be resolved by changing your vibe.

# Raising Your Vibe Through Gratitude

I served as Board President to a large progressive church in Massachusetts for several years. During one particularly challenging time, the board members were concerned about being able to maintain the level of service our church was offering due to not having enough money, staffing, or other resources to achieve our strategic objectives. The vibe in the room was heavy. Yet before the meeting began, we enjoyed a delicious potluck dinner that included healthy vegetarian fare, with chocolate dipped strawberries, fresh salads, and a vast array of foods to please any palate. The church was filled with extraordinarily beautiful artwork, most of which had been created and donated by congregants. The sound booth and music center had contemporary equipment and excellent technology to enable live streaming of our services and creation of astounding music week after week. I asked the board to look around them and tell me what they saw. At first, they didn't have any idea what I was asking, so I mentioned the things I listed here. "We are so incredibly blessed with abundance and yet what we are focusing on is the feeling of lack," I told them. They immediately resonated with this notion. Were we going to focus on what we were missing or on the many blessings right in front of us?

Benedictine monk, author, and teacher Brother David Steindal-Rast is the founder of the Network for Grateful Living. His TED talk on gratitude has been viewed nearly six million times. His primary message is that while we might think that happy people are more grateful, his research has shown that it is the other way around. Gratitude is a cornerstone of happiness. Being grateful for what one has, rather than disgruntled with what you do not have, elevates your vibe.

What does gratitude have to do with increasing your financial freedom? Everything. Gratitude is a high vibe state. The more you cultivate an attitude of gratitude, the more you will be creating a high vibe for your life. That creates a positive feedback loop where your attitude of gratitude raises your vibe, and having a higher vibe lends toward being more grateful.

A study at the National Academy of Sciences found that grateful people advance further in their careers, are less materialistic and earn more money. This research validates the premise of this book that living in with an elevated vibe leads to greater financial success.

Here are some simple ways to enhance your ability to experience and express gratitude:

1.  Compliment people as often as you can. When I am at a coffee shop, I express something positive about the person waiting on me. "Thank you for making my day a little nicer" or "I appreciate your smile this morning" are simple ways to not only raise the vibe of those around you, but to train yourself in noticing positive aspects of others.

2.  At family mealtimes, have everyone recall a few things from their day or week for which they are grateful.

3.  When going for a walk or a run, go through the alphabet and find something that you are grateful for with each corresponding letter. I do this when I would go for a run – because I hate running! So instead of allowing my mind to wallow in

negative thinking about how much I am not enjoying the run, I train my mind to do this exercise. A: I am grateful for appreciating life, B: I am grateful for broccoli and eating well, C: I am grateful to have a cat that sits on my lap every day, D: I am grateful for this day and so on. It is a fun way to raise your vibe anytime that you find yourself dipping into negativity.

4.  Practice gratitude for everything you touch as you do your morning routine. Be grateful for a warm bed, a hot shower, clean clothes, food in your cabinets, and a car to drive. You could start your day complaining that the bed is old, you don't like your clothes, you need to go grocery shopping but don't have time and your car is run down. It is all a matter of perspective, which is based on your BEAT, which can be trained and elevated.

5.  Keep a gratitude journal. I have kept a gratitude journal for over a decade, and I promise you, it is a very impactful practice. It takes me less than 5 minutes to jot down 10-15 things I am grateful for each day, but the overall impact on training myself to focus on the blessings in my life is tremendous.

Take a moment right now as part of your exercises in this book to write down five or ten things in your life for which you are grateful. Better still, share it with the Vibe Tribe group on Facebook! Do it now! You don't elevate your vibe by thinking you should. You elevate your vibe by taking thinking different thoughts and taking different actions.

# FACTOR THREE: YOUR BEAT:

# Beliefs, Emotions, Attitudes, Thoughts

# CHAPTER 6

# The Seat of Your BEAT: Beliefs

*No one is ready for a thing, until he believes he can acquire it.*
*The state of mind must be BELIEF, not mere hope or wish.*
*— Napoleon Hill*

I recently watched a webinar by a wealthy, successful entrepreneur named Dean Graziosi. He was touting the benefits of real estate investing and selling an online course that teaches people how to create multiple real estate deals per month. Dean is an amazing man. His energy and passion for helping people is infectious. As I watched the webinar and read the comments people were making, I knew Dean would crush it with sales from this advertising webinar, and kudos to him. He is selling something that he believes in, and it will likely help some people.

But I also just shook my head as I clicked the webinar off. I thought, "That's great information, but if people don't change their Money Vibe, their lives will never change. They may make some money, but without addressing their fundamental beliefs about money, they will repeat the same experiences over and over."

The National Endowment for Financial Education found that 70 percent of lottery winners end up broke in a few years. That seems impossible, but such research has been repeated and verified numerous times. People repeatedly create external conditions in their lives that validate what they believe.

We have spent a good deal of time in this book so far talking about your BEAT – your Beliefs, Emotions, Attitudes, and Thoughts. It is time to go one step further and understand that it is your beliefs that are the underpinning and driver of the rest of your vibe.

Beliefs create the infrastructure of how you see and interact with the world. They are thoughts and feelings that you have held for so long, often without conscious consent, that they resonate as true for you. The problem is that many of your beliefs are not true or false; they are simply the way you have come to construct your worldview.

This year the east coast was hit by severe hurricanes with Hurricane Harvey pummeling Texas and Hurricane Irma following close behind wreaking havoc on the coast of Florida. Some "televangelists" touted that these storms were God's wrath on America for allowing gay people to legally marry in our country. Is that true? Is it not true? Many people believe it's true, while others believe otherwise. The same principle applies regarding your beliefs about yourself, life, money, earning, success, and a myriad of other things. What is "true" for you is what you believe.

In this section of the book, you will again employ detailed inventories to help ascertain your beliefs. In many ways, working at the level of belief is much easier than the all-too-common psychological paradigm that posits that you must discover the root of what ails you, and that, due to some events that fundamentally scarred you for life, this root rests somewhere in your unconscious mind. That is a belief – and it is one to which I no longer subscribe. Once you identify the beliefs that underlie what is limiting you, you can change. It requires persistence and practice, but you can transform your beliefs to more empowering ones. "Oh, wow, that's a silly belief, and it's not even true! It is just what I have believed all these years!" Then apply the 3 C's process (Catch It, Challenge It, Change It) and earnestly focus on your desires and vision.

The problem is that so many of your beliefs have become so ingrained in you that you no longer even notice them. Let me give you an example.

I moved into a new home in Washington, D.C., not long ago and when our moving cube arrived, neighbors graciously came to help us unload. We have one particularly large, beautiful piece of furniture that is striking in its design and color - a bright red antique bookcase from Indonesia. We finished unloading, and I unwrapped it from the protective covering. My new neighbor, Deb, said, "Wow, that is stunning! I have never seen a piece like that before," to which I responded, "Thank you! I am so lucky to have a good friend who is a furniture dealer. He spotted this for me at an auction. I was able to get it for only $400!"

Later that week I was teaching my Money Vibe live webinar. It occurred to me that I felt self-conscious having this piece of furniture that looks quite exquisite and expensive. I was afraid my new neighbors might not like me if they assessed that I have a lot of money.

That fear – "She won't like me if she thinks I have money" – never occurred to my conscious mind until I was teaching the class. It was driven by a belief that some people don't like people who "have money" or seem to be from a higher socioeconomic class. If you would have asked me if I held any concern that people wouldn't like me because of having money, I would have said, "No, of course not!" But there it was, running in the background and expressed as a minimizing, dismissive comment so that I felt more secure.

Once I uncovered that unsupportive belief, I immediately practiced my three-step process. I CAUGHT the belief that was driving what I said to my neighbor (i.e., people won't like me if they think I have more money than they do). Then I CHALLENGED the belief by talking back to it (i.e., "Is that accurate? Is that what you want to believe? Does that belief empower you in any way?"). Then I CHANGED the belief by seeing what I wanted to experience (i.e., laughing and enjoying time with my new neighbors, feeling appreciation for the friend who found this beautiful piece for me and feeling grateful that it now graces my living room! I also appreciated myself for creating a Money Vibe that allows me to bring beautiful aesthetics into my home with ease when I am clear on what I desire.

I love this process and the freedom it brings. In this example I am free to own beautiful things and have friends enjoy and appreciate them. I can enhance their appreciation by being gracious and accepting the compliment and praise. This story is a small example that creates a new world of opportunity and experience.

Let's look at another example to drill this home, and then we will turn toward beginning to uncover some of your core beliefs. Years ago, a friend of mine kept reaching out to me to ask my advice about a program she was creating at her workplace. After the fourth or fifth time she called me, it dawned on me that I could be an asset to the project she was working on, so I said, "Hey, this sounds like fun. Why don't you hire me to do this project for you?"

As I relayed this story to various friends over the next weeks and months, most of them were astounded that I was so direct and straightforward in suggesting my friend hire me.

I was flabbergasted. Why wouldn't I ask? It sounded like a fun project, and I did possess the requisite knowledge and experience that would elevate the success of the program.

Seeing my friends' reactions, I dug into what belief I held that allowed me with such ease and comfort to ask for the work. What I realized is that I wasn't attached to her answer at all. I didn't need the work, but if I could help her, I was happy to figure out how to fit it into my schedule. If she said, "No, thanks," I would not have felt hurt or embarrassed in any way. I believe in the importance of service – making a difference where I can with what I know. Lastly, I believe in synchronicity – that when things show up at the right time and in the right way, they will work out.

My friend never expected that I had the time to take on such a large-scale project, so she hadn't bothered to ask me. When I told her I could make it work if she could come up with the necessary funds, she said she would investigate it and get back to me. The following month, I started an enjoyable and meaningful consulting gig that ended up lasting ten years. I am glad I held the beliefs I did so that I wasn't afraid to ask!

Play that same scenario out differently. Suppose I believed that it is not appropriate to ask for work or offer my services. If I held the belief that people will ask if they want me to work for them, I would never have asked my friend, she would never have gotten my input on the project, and perhaps the project wouldn't have taken off as well as it did. In fact, it is a service program that is still running nearly 20 years later. I would not have made that money, nor would I have met that network of people. All these events occurred because of one belief. Your beliefs determine everything.

Here are some of the many ways false, limiting beliefs impact your life:

- Not applying for a new job or a promotion because you believe you're too old, too inexperienced, too shy or just not the right fit.

- Believing you are only complete or successful if you are married, have a child, earn a million dollars, get a Ph.D., or any other external marker that validates your worth.

- Not writing the book, starting the blog, or starting that social group you have long wanted to do because you believe you will be negatively judged.

- Believing that you should relegate your desires and wishes to the sidelines in service of others.

- Believing that you "don't have time" to work on a project that you have long wanted to do.

- Believing you must own a house or have your house in a certain look and feel in order to entertain guests.

- Believing you will never be happy again after the loss of a relationship or job.

- Believing you cannot ask for a raise because that means "X" about you, your integrity, or your relationship with your boss.

- Believing that it takes money to make money.

Each one of these examples is derived from a real-life experience I have had with a coaching client or student in my programs. I could write a whole book of limiting beliefs and how they restrict our success and happiness!

Every time I teach a seminar on Money Vibe people want to jump right into what they can do to bring more money into their lives. I appreciate that energy and motivation but changing actions without altering beliefs will only lead to more frustration.

The most important task of bringing more money into your life is to uncover every limiting belief you have about money, earning and investing, and turn it into a conviction that empowers you and is aligned with your desires. Robert Kiyosaki, the author of Rich Dad, Poor Dad posted on Facebook: "The number one question asked this week was how to start investing with little or no money. Please hear this, as this is the hardest thing for people to understand: you do NOT invest with money! You invest with your mind! No matter what the field, your biggest asset is your mind."

# Stop Asking Why!

One of my Money Vibe students, Noreen, called me a month or so ago to discuss an area where she felt stuck. She said that she repeatedly goes through "feast or famine" cycles in her business. She will have more work than she can manage for a period, and then work dries up and she goes into a panic that she won't be able to support herself.

"I'd like to know why I keep doing this repeatedly. Why do I have these incredible cycles and end up worrying so much? I lose sleep over it, I end up getting all upset, and then before I know it, the work starts rolling again. But the next time a dry spell comes, I go right back into fear. I want to know why I do that!"

"You are asking the wrong question," I told her.

"What do you mean? I need to get underneath this and understand it. I have to figure out why I do this so I can stop the pattern. I either need to interrupt the cycle and have a steadier stream of work, or I need to stop freaking out every time a dip in the cycle occurs," she exclaimed with exasperation in her voice.

"How long have you been trying to figure this out," I queried?

"Well, I guess for as long as I have been in business."

"And have you figured it out yet?"

She laughed. "No, that's why I am calling you!"

"Noreen, maybe there's nothing to 'figure out.' Maybe all you need to do is to understand what you believe that has you go through these cycles. When you are in the 'up' side of the cycle and crazy busy with work, what do you believe during those times? What belief underlies that process?"

"I believe that I can't keep up and that the quality of my work will suffer," came her disheartened reply.

"Yes, understood. And what about when you are in the 'down' side of the cycle and there is not enough work coming in. What do you believe then?"

"I believe that I won't be able to support myself, that my business is going to fail, and that I will end up homeless or something!"

We both chuckled in understanding and sympathy for her plight.

"Yes, okay, and how many years have you been in business?"

"Seventeen," she replied.

"Have you ever gone a full year without earning anything?"

"Oh, God, no!" she exclaimed with mild horror.

"Okay, and what about a full quarter? Have you ever gone an entire quarter with no work?"

"No, I haven't."

"So, is your belief valid?"

"No, it's not," she said with calm recognition. "But how do I change it? How do I stop believing, thinking and feeling this way?"

"You just started the process right now by identifying the limiting belief, and we just disempowered it by your ability to answer these questions. Now, let me ask you one more thing. Is this what you want to experience?"

"No! Of course not!"

"Great, then what do you want to experience? What is possible? What is your highest vision?"

"I want a steady flow of work - not on crazy overload, but not down to nothing either."

"Great! So, if you were to experience a slow-down again, what could you choose to believe?"

"Well, I could decide to believe that things will pick up again because they always do. I could also believe that I need the time to reconnect with former clients and nurture those relationships so that I have a steady stream of work. I could be grateful for the chance to work on my skills so that I am continuing to improve what I offer my clients!" The relief in her voice was palpable.

"Yes, you could. How do those beliefs feel?"

"They feel great. They do!"

"Great! Now your job is to practice these new beliefs until they become second nature to you, so you 'own them' as yours. All it takes is practicing this three-step formula every time a disempowering belief emerges. It does not change overnight. It's almost like working a new muscle. The first day you go to the gym, you don't run a marathon or lift your body weight. But in time, you can build up to those things. The same goes with changing your beliefs."

"Who knew it could be so easy? I thought I had to dig into my psyche and understand the roots of my fears and limiting beliefs."

"Nope. That was just another limiting belief!" We both laughed.

Months later I ran into Noreen at a social event, and she told me she no longer needed to "practice" the new belief, that it was now second nature to her – it was her new belief system. She told me how she had already transferred this practice to different areas where she had other limiting beliefs. It was becoming a way of life for her. Rather than asking why, she had learned to ask, "What do I believe about this situation that is causing my difficulty?" This question works in relationships when you feel slighted or upset by someone. It works when you are worried about your health, finances, or a new project. When you feel anxious, afraid, or confused in any way, just ask yourself, "What do I believe that has me feeling this way?"

As I do this work with hundreds of people each year, I see that most of our discomfort comes down to two fundamental beliefs: 1. There won't be enough, and 2. I am not sufficient. There won't be enough money, time, love, care, pleasure or whatever; and I am not something enough – I am not smart enough, good enough, old enough, young enough, experienced enough, sexy enough. Whatever the case may be, the key angst people struggle with is "not enough-ness."

A Money Vibe student, Brock, said during one session that he needed help because he was "stuck" and could not bring in the money he needed to be earning to sustain his lifestyle. I asked him what he meant by stuck to which he replied, "I don't know. I just seem to have some block that is keeping me from bringing in money. I have had a couple of opportunities for contracts lately, but they don't get completed. I wish I understood why this happens to me and why I feel so inept financially."

I said, "So you believe you are stuck, and you have some block?"

"Yes, I do."

"Instead of asking why you feel this way, you want to uncover the belief that is keeping you stuck. Okay, so you can see the belief. That's the first step. Now, does it support you and is it the belief you want to maintain?" I asked. While I know the answer to these questions, there is something powerful about having people say it, and for them to hear it said so concretely and explicitly. The ego likes to confound things.

One of the ways to interrupt the power of the ego is to state things so stupidly simple that it breaks through the confusion.

"No," Brock retorted. "It does not support me, and I do not want to continue believing that. I'm not even sure I believe it."

"Well, it is what you said to me, so on some level, you believe that is the case. There is some mysterious block you have that is making you stuck. Sounds kind of silly, now, right?"

Laughing, he acknowledged it did.

"Great, let's get to the work of changing it then. So, is it true that you have a block?"

"It feels like I do," he said with resignation.

"Yes, I understand that. But is there a block in front of you right now? Can you see a block outside your window? Is there a block on your computer?"

Again, laughing, and perhaps a bit exasperated, he said, "No, not at all."

"Right, so is it true that you have a block?"

"I guess it's only true in my mind," he said.

"Correct. So, let's remove it. You can see the limiting belief, and you know that it is not true. So now is the fun part. How do you want to feel? What is your highest vision for how you can feel about earning, garnering contracts and about your career?"

"I want to feel confident that I have the power and control over my financial life. I want to feel good about my work."

"Yes, right. And when you feel good about your career, and feel powerful about your financial life, what would you be doing?"

"Well, I would be in the lab, doing experiments, seeing results… and getting paid!" The shift in Brock's voice was palpable. He was upbeat, energized and filled with optimism and clarity.

"Great. So, can that be your new belief? Right now, not tomorrow, not when you 'remove some block' but right now, can you believe you are powerful and in control of your finances, regardless of what is happening with your contract work?"

"Yes, I can!"

"That is awesome. Then your work moving forward from this point on is to keep seeing and saying this new belief. Feel it in your energy. Feel the confidence, the relief, and the enjoyment. This belief can be your new truth."

While this may sound like I am making this next part up to make a great story for my book, I promise you it is true. Within a week, Brock secured a new contract with a lab he had worked with previously, and within another couple of weeks, another opportunity came his way. His career was back on track. He felt powerful, in control and happy with his career and financial life. And so can you!

# Uncovering Your Beliefs

Your beliefs, BEAT, and vibe about money often determine the amount of wealth you acquire and how you feel about it. Therefore, delving into your money beliefs is the essential next step for moving you closer to the financial life you envision. Are you willing to believe that you can have a radically different economic future? Can you believe you can be a millionaire? Multi-millionaire? Do you believe there is a connection between your outer life and your inner vibe? Do you believe you can be a force for good, contributing significant amounts of money to causes that you support? Many people today believe that being in debt is just a part of life and that they are powerless to overcome the cycle of overspending. Do you hold such a belief? If so, you must transform for it to know financial freedom.

Let's go deeper to start weeding out the specifics of your limiting money beliefs. I am just going to assume that you have limiting money beliefs because most people do! Even when a person has sufficient financial means, as many of my coaching clients do, I still see a general vibe of lack of freedom.

Below are two self-assessment inventories designed to delve deeper into the beliefs you hold about money. These questions ask you to reflect on what you think and believe, not on your actual outer circumstances or experience. In each inventory, rate your experience of each statement on a scale of 0 to 5. Zero means that you never or almost never believe this way, and five represents that you always or almost always believe that to be true. The top set of statements reflects higher vibe beliefs, whereas the second group reflects those with a lower money vibe.

You may be inclined to make your score look better than it is. That is human nature. (Most people rate themselves as being an above average driver while rating others as being below average!) But remember, this assessment is just for you. The key here is awareness and greater understanding of your BEAT.

| HIGH VIBE STATEMENTS | LESS   MORE |
| --- | --- |
| Money is everywhere and I can direct the flow of money currency into my life. | 0 1 2 3 4 5 |
| I enjoy money, making, saving, and investing it. | 0 1 2 3 4 5 |
| It is easy to make money. | 0 1 2 3 4 5 |
| I love making money and what it brings into my life. | 0 1 2 3 4 5 |
| I have enough self-worth to be comfortable having a lot of money without worrying what others may think. | 0 1 2 3 4 5 |
| My finances are secure. | 0 1 2 3 4 5 |
| Money gives me opportunities. | 0 1 2 3 4 5 |
| The more money I have, the more I can do to help others. | 0 1 2 3 4 5 |
| There is financial opportunity everywhere. I just have to decide in what way I want to make money. | 0 1 2 3 4 5 |
| I love being around wealthy people. | 0 1 2 3 4 5 |
| Money flows into my life easily. | 0 1 2 3 4 5 |
| I've done well financially so far in life. | 0 1 2 3 4 5 |
| I can trust myself when it comes to money and financial decisions. | 0 1 2 3 4 5 |

| HIGH VIBE STATEMENTS | LESS   MORE |
|---|---|
| I believe in the importance of wise money management. | 0 1 2 3 4 5 |
| I value having money. | 0 1 2 3 4 5 |
| I live in an abundant universe. | 0 1 2 3 4 5 |
| I feel sufficient when it comes to money. | 0 1 2 3 4 5 |
| I feel abundant when it comes to money. | 0 1 2 3 4 5 |
| I feel optimistic about my financial future. | 0 1 2 3 4 5 |
| I am generally relaxed and at ease when it comes to money. | 0 1 2 3 4 5 |
| Total Score: | _____ /100 |

| LOW VIBE STATEMENTS | LESS   MORE |
|---|---|
| It's hard to earn money. | 0 1 2 3 4 5 |
| I am in survival mode, living day-to-day. | 0 1 2 3 4 5 |
| I'm just not good with money so it's tough to have enough to feel comfortable. | 0 1 2 3 4 5 |
| I worry about money. | 0 1 2 3 4 5 |
| I can't save or get ahead. | 0 1 2 3 4 5 |
| I hate thinking about money. | 0 1 2 3 4 5 |
| Thinking about money or my financial life makes me feel badly about myself. | 0 1 2 3 4 5 |

| LOW VIBE STATEMENTS | LESS MORE |
|---|---|
| Money is not that important. It's "only money." | 0 1 2 3 4 5 |
| Money is the root of all evil. | 0 1 2 3 4 5 |
| I had better hold onto the money I have. | 0 1 2 3 4 5 |
| It is inappropriate to talk about money to friends or colleagues. | 0 1 2 3 4 5 |
| I keep thinking things will get easier for me financially, but it never seems to change. | 0 1 2 3 4 5 |
| People won't like or accept me if they feel I have more money than they do. | 0 1 2 3 4 5 |
| I have a block about money. | 0 1 2 3 4 5 |
| It takes money to make money. | 0 1 2 3 4 5 |
| Money does not bring happiness. | 0 1 2 3 4 5 |
| It is not right for me to have more when other people have so little. | 0 1 2 3 4 5 |
| If I make a lot of money, it will change my personality and values. | 0 1 2 3 4 5 |
| I worry that I won't have enough money in my senior years or to be able to retire. | 0 1 2 3 4 5 |
| Thinking too much about money or trying to be wealthy means that I am greedy and self-centered. | 0 1 2 3 4 5 |
| Total Score: | ____ /100 |

**Scoring:**

- If you scored 80 or above on the High Vibe Statements and 20 or below on the Low Vibe Statements, congratulations! You have a **very high Money Vibe**!

- If you scored 70 or above on the High Vibe Statements and 30 or below on the Low Vibe Statements, congratulations! You have a **high Money Vibe!**

- If you scored 60 or above on the High Vibe Statements and 40 or below on the Low Vibe Statements, congratulations! You have a **healthy Money Vibe!**

- If you scored 50 or above on the High Vibe Statements and 50 or below on the Low Vibe Statements, keep working on this program! You are **nearing a healthy Money Vibe!**

- If you scored 50 or below on the High Vibe Statements and 50 or above on the Low Vibe Statements, your Money Vibe is **not supportive of changing your financial future.**

Commit to working this program more intensely over the next year to develop a healthy, robust, and supportive Money Vibe!

# High Money Vibe™ Beliefs

The Dalai Lama stated in an interview for *Market Watch* magazine that, "Money is good. It is important. Without money, daily survival -- not to mention further development -- is impossible. We are not even questioning its importance. At the same time, it is wrong to consider money a god or a substance endowed with some power of its own. To think that money is everything, and that just by having lots of it all our problems will be solved is a serious mistake. The mind is key. If anything should be considered a god, so to speak, it is the mind, not money. A healthy, positive mind is the utmost priority." That is a powerful statement and one that inspires me about my work with you in this book and my commitment to the Money Vibe movement. I am passionate about helping people get the "money monkeys" off their backs, and to feel powerful, free, and peaceful about money. I want to see people lit up about their work and service to the world.

Jack Canfield, author of the *Chicken Soup for the Soul* series, believes you must decide to be rich and then spend your entire life fulfilling that decision. Deciding to be rich was an important decision for him given that before becoming a multi-millionaire with his book series he received at least 144 rejection letters from publishers. But because of his unwavering belief in his ability to be wealthy, Jack never veered from his commitment. He believes you need to have a clear mental picture of the life you will lead when you have wealth and then spend time every day seeing that mental image in your mind.

Author and multimillionaire real estate investor, Dr. David Ryback, believes that the secret to wealth lies in non-attachment. On his way to millions his focus was on making intelligent choices regarding how he saved and invested money, and he focused on being of service to others. His book, *Secrets of a Zen Millionaire*, is filled with wisdom about the importance of service, mindfulness, compassion, and prudence on the way to wealth. Far too often, however, people are deeply attached to their beliefs as being gospel truth. Try convincing someone that their deeply held beliefs are simply thoughts and feelings that have congealed into a worldview! It is not an easy task. Notice your own attachment to what you believe about yourself and the world. Anytime you are resistant or afraid to initiate change, what underlies that fear is some belief that is holding you back.

My personal money beliefs are spiritual in nature because I believe that the highest form of life mastery is when you are doing what you love and contributing to the greater good of humanity, while simultaneously being deeply aware and in control of your inner domain of BEAT, which creates your vibe. Below is my Money Vibe Manifesto that outlines my core beliefs about money.

# Money Vibe™ Manifesto

1. I believe that everything is energy, including money. The more I consciously align myself with the flow of Life energy, the more I create the conditions for sufficiency, inflow, peace, and joy.

2. I am one with the creative universal energy and therefore I always have enough of what I need, and I happily share my abundance with others.

3. I believe in myself. I trust myself to make prudent decisions, to be a responsible steward of all that Life brings my way, to pay attention to my financial fitness, and to conduct myself in a way that honors the universal life force within me.

4. I believe in the power of creative imagination, and that thoughts and emotions create. Therefore, I do not dwell on any negative, fearful feeling or thought.

5. I believe I am here to grow and that my life unfolds according to my vibe. Therefore, I align with high vibe energy through my Beliefs, Emotions, Attitudes, and Thoughts (BEAT).

6. I believe in being of service. Therefore, I offer the best of myself in all I do.

7. I believe persistence is a virtue worth cultivating. Therefore, I embrace challenges and opportunities as they arise. I envision my highest good and persist in my beliefs and actions toward the manifestation of my desires.

8. I believe manifesting my deepest desires is a calling, that it is the highest way to live and one to which I devote my life.

These are not the "right" beliefs to hold. They do not have magical power. But holding these beliefs, or something of a similar high vibe, coupled with clear, decisive, committed action, leads to untold financial success, satisfaction, and happiness. It is this intersection of BEAT and ACTION that leads to mastery of life. I choose to cultivate beliefs that support my vision and desires – and I invite you to do the same.

Take the time to write the first draft of your Money Vibe Manifesto or adopt this one as your own. Your beliefs can be consciously created rather than unconsciously inherited and assumed. Without knowing what you want to experience and create, all of this is for naught. Every concept in this book gears you toward one thing: bringing into existence the life you want to have with financial abundance, greater happiness, deeper fulfillment, and wellbeing.

# CHAPTER 7

# Align Your Actions with Your Financial Values

*When your values are clear to you,*
*making decisions becomes easier.*
*— Roy E. Disney*

I feel so blessed to be able to spend my summers in the Thousand Islands of Upstate New York, living in the cottage that was built by my ancestors on property that has been in my family for six generations. The area is very rural; life is straightforward and slow. The St. Lawrence River is the focal point of the area, connecting the Atlantic Ocean to the Great Lakes. Ships and freighters meander through the islands reminding us of distant lands far and foreign to this quaint existence. I enjoy the summer months here like a deep exhale after an intense workout.

I recently ran into an old friend of mine from my school days during the 4th of July festivities in my hometown. While we were catching up, she mentioned that she would be retiring and moving to Florida for the winters this coming year. Realizing that she is only a couple of years older than I am, I responded with muted amazement at her ability to retire so young. She never went to college and, from what I knew from the times we had seen one another over the years, she had always worked at the local central school doing custodial work and driving the school bus.

"You're retiring?" I asked with apparent surprise. "You are so young! How are you retiring already?"

"Yeah," she said. "I know I'm lucky, but I have my 30 years in at the school, so I took early retirement. We saved up over the years, so we could do this. I don't want to have to work my entire life. We enjoy Florida. The weather is great. After we paid off our house, we bought a small place down there and have been paying it off over the past 15 years."

My mind was reeling by this point. She owns two homes free and clear? She has no college degree, no real "career track" in the traditional sense, and yet here she is retiring at 55 and living between her hometown in the north and a place in the south!

"We were very clear on what we value," she said of her and her husband. "We watched our parents work themselves to death. We wanted an easier life, so we lived very simply, paid for everything with cash, put money into retirement and paid off the house as soon as we could. We don't like the feeling of debt hanging over our heads. And we love Florida, so we just stayed focused on what we valued and wanted, and well, here we are! I'll be done with work in less than a year!"

There is an excellent formula for financial freedom! Be clear on what you value, establish what it is you want, stay focused, and take action. Boom!

There is a lot to garner from this story. What does it cost to sustain an upper-middle-class lifestyle with nice cars, a big home, fancy clothing, and exotic vacations? And how much money does it require to maintain a modest, working-class lifestyle? That is not to say you shouldn't aspire to higher levels of performance and career success if that is what you value. But be clear on what you value and where you want to go instead of engaging in the mindless consumption of "more, more, more" that you are spoon-fed by our culture. There is beauty and power in simplicity.

Far too often, when I ask people about their financial values, they have no idea how to respond. Acquiring money for its own sake is shallow and empty. But creating wealth to support your values is vibrant, exciting, and fulfilling and creates a life of meaning.

Do you know why you want more money? Knowing your "compelling why" for creating financial success will inspire and motivate you to stay the course even when things do not turn out as you wish or planned. Let your "why" be your guide. Your financial values should form the roots of your financial goals.

Give this some thought and then do the writing exercises below. These questions may feel redundant but answer them anyway and see what themes emerge.

I want more money because:

_____

_____

_____

I want more money to be able to:

_____

_____

_____

When I have more money, I will:

_____

_____

_____

What did you see? Were there things that appeared in your answers that had to do with feeling a certain way? If you wrote anything related to feeling less stress, more confident, less worried, and so forth, do you realize that you can feel that way right now? Anything you are feeling stems from what you believe, and you can change your beliefs with focus, consistency, and practice.

Take the next step now to declare your financial values. Rank each value below according to its importance to you. Place the items that have the greatest meaning to you at the top of the list and those that are not important or less important to you at the bottom. Do this in rank number order.

You will find that after you get past the first three or four items, the others get a little less clear. Feel free to go to the bottom of the list and indicate those that you know are not a priority for you. For example, when I did this exercise, I knew that social status was not part of my "compelling why," so after listing my top values, I placed social status at the bottom to help me eliminate some of the choices. Take your time. Think this through and enjoy a few moments of reflection.

* Legacy (Leaving money or possessions to others)

* Impact (Impacting social, political, or environmental movements or other large-scale projects)

* Adventure (Travel, learning)

* Security

* Charitable giving (Causes you wish to support)

* Social status

* Time freedom (Able to choose what to do, when and where)

* Generosity (Helping others, giving your money to family and friends)

* Peace of mind

* Sufficiency (Having enough)

* Abundance (Having more than enough)

* Wealth (Having more than enough for lifetimes)

* Health and wellness pursuits

* Beauty and aesthetics

* Other _____

# My Financial Values Ranking

1. _____

2. _____

3. _____

4. _____

5. _____

6. _____

7. _____

8. _____

9. _____

10. _____

11. _____

12. _____

13. _____

14. _____

From this list, write down your top five values and then make your financial decisions aligned with these. Commit these five values to memory. Let them serve as your guide each time you spend money or make a purchase. Ask yourself to reflect on whether this acquisition aligns with one of your five values. If not, don't spend the money. Do this as an experiment for a month with your Money Vibe Partner and share each week what you notice. When your actions are aligned with your values, you are living with a deep sense of internal integrity.

My Financial Values are:

1. _____

2. _____

3. _____

4. _____

5. _____

People often ask me if they should put away their money and save for the future or enjoy today. The question always strikes me as unusual because it sets up a false dichotomy. It is not helpful to have an "either/or" relationship with money. Instead, I suggest you develop a "both/and" vibe. The answer to that important question is: Do both! Enjoy your money by investing it in things that bring joy now while simultaneously creating a prudent investment plan that addresses your future.

When you start thinking in terms of investing money according to your values and being sure that all your values are addressed, you gain tremendous clarity with regard to your financial life.

Never think in terms of *spending* money. Always think in terms of investing it. I purchased a pumpkin spice coffee this morning. Did I *spend* that $3? No! I *invested* it in the simple pleasure of a good cup of coffee. Do I spend money on tuition for my son? Not at all! I am *investing* in his future in a way that is aligned with my values around education and maximizing potential.

As you start thinking in terms of investing your money with every financial transaction, you will probably make different decisions. Do you really want to invest your money in a new purse or piece of sports gear or new pair of shoes? If so, what value are you expressing? Pay attention to the ways that you use money. Stop engaging in "retail therapy" as a form of entertainment.

One of the most prudent ways to develop wealth is consistently having more inflow than outflow of money and using the excess to build more wealth. You will never be able to do that if you *spend* every dollar you earn.

Robert Kiyosaki wrote, "The rich get richer by reinvesting asset profits back into assets." Most people don't make money work for them. When you have a spending mindset, you probably will never learn to do so. Cultivating an investing mindset means that you think about how to make money work for you.

# FACTOR FOUR:
# Focus and Desire

# CHAPTER 8

# Designing Your Financial Future

*Success, like happiness, cannot be pursued; it must ensue, and it only does so as the unintended side effect of one's personal dedication to a cause greater than oneself...*
*— Viktor Frankl, Man's Search for Meaning*

I attended a wonderfully inspiring church in northeast Massachusetts for over 15 years. A light-filled sanctuary with large windows overlooks a saltwater river and the surrounding trees. The energy is electric with upbeat music, beautiful décor, and engaged, enthusiastic people. The minister at the time was a small sprite of a woman, full of passion and zeal. She delivered powerful messages week after week, often donning an Irish brogue or the voice of Yoda to highlight her talks.

After attending the church for a few years and felt an intense calling to do something different with my career. At the time, I was 20-plus years into a career as a psychotherapist as well as having a thriving professional coaching practice, and it was going quite well. I enjoyed the work, was respected in my community, and business was steady. Yet I felt restless, like there was something more that wanted to come through me. I had long felt the desire to be a speaker and author teaching empowerment programs, but ten years prior when I set out to do that work, I had failed miserably. I was in no hurry to repeat that experience.

One Sunday, the minister, Reverend Shipley Allinson, spoke on the role and nature of desire in our lives. I listened transfixed by her message. She spoke with clarity and passion about how our deepest desires – those that won't go away and persist in us over time – are part of our life purpose and how it is our spiritual duty to fulfill them. She said the word itself – desire, or de-sire – means "of the Father." The persistent yearning in our heart reflects a spiritual calling that supports the forward evolution of our world. The more we each connect with and express our desires; the more humanity evolves toward higher and higher levels.

She referenced the Gnostic Gospel of Thomas: "If you bring forth what is within you, what you bring forth will save you. If you do not bring forth what is within you, what you do not bring forth will destroy you." That message resonated deeply in my heart and soul.

That was how I felt – that the longer I ignored the calling to speak, teach and write, the more I was slowly dying inside. I don't mean literal death, but the joy of life, vitality, and enthusiasm was waning in me. What I was not bringing forth was destroying me. I could see it so clearly after hearing that frame. Until that moment, I had restlessness in my heart and soul but had no language for how to understand or express what was happening to me. I resolved at that moment to face my fears and get into action toward my long-held dream.

Within the year, I had designed and delivered the first of many empowerment programs I have created over the years. Since then, I have authored three books, written chapters in several others, and spoken to thousands of people as an empowerment speaker. And I Love What I Do!! It is deeply a "Self-expression" for me. Writing, speaking, teaching classes, and watching my student's lives transform right before my eyes is the most fulfilling thing I can imagine doing.

Oh, and the money? I continue to be profoundly grateful and humbled that people pay me to provide work that I deeply love. Yes, I am proud to say that I make a terrific income while fulfilling my desires. There is nothing like it.

I am passionate about helping other people find that same connection because I believe it is a process of spiritual growth and part of the evolution of humanity. Too often people are uncertain whether their desires represent a passion or a passing fancy. There are ways to know.

Desire, as I am using the word, is not a whim, or fleeting idea. It is not what other people tell you to do. And it is not our cultural narrative about success. What will fulfill you at the deepest level is bringing forth who you are into the world in the most real, powerful, and substantive way.

Desire is a profound and persistent urge to move toward and create or express something. It is a force that has vibrant and creative energy. It often is frightening because most often you cannot see how the desire will unfold. The most important thing for you to understand is that how it will unfold is none of your business! Your desire is your business.

I have been a full-time author and speaker for six years, and as I move forward with my business and take actions aligned with my values and desires, things organically unfold. I have found truth in the famous quote by William Hutchinson Murray in his writing about the Scottish Himalayan expedition:

"Until one is committed, there is hesitancy, the chance to draw back — concerning all acts of initiative (and creation), there is one elementary the ignorance of which kills countless ideas and splendid plans: that the moment one definitely commits oneself, then Providence moves too. All sorts of things occur to help one that would never otherwise have occurred. A whole stream of events issues from the decision, raising in one's favor all manner of unforeseen incidents and meetings and material assistance, which no man could have dreamed would have come his way.

Whatever you can do, or dream you can do, begin it. Boldness has genius, power, and magic in it. Begin it now."

When you are committed and begin to act, "Providence moves!"

A desire for something, whether it is a new job, a change in career, a new relationship, or a new financial experience in life, only occurs because you are ready to grow to the next level of your evolution. You are willing to raise your vibe.

Many people think that money will give them something – a feeling or experience they desire — whether it is freedom from worry, or enhanced self-esteem or security. They believe that money will grant this wish. The truth is that money does not automatically fulfill your needs or give you the feelings you want. Think about it. You probably earn more money now than you did ten years ago, and yet you are still fraught with the same inner experience and turmoil that you had before.

Rather than viewing money as an end, come to see it as a medium of the game you are playing to demonstrate your growth in consciousness. The more you elevate your money vibe, the more you will bring money into your life, and the greater peace of mind you will have – not because of the money, but because you will now have an unflappable confidence and sense of your ability to manage life itself.

With clarity about what you desire, the willingness and ability to move forward toward your desires, take prudent action and hold high vibe beliefs, you will see financial reward. Here is a formula for financial success:

## CLARITY + PRUDENT ACTION (ALIGNED WITH YOUR VALUES) + HIGH VIBE = RESULTS

When you are unclear about what you desire, you will spend your entire life living by default. Consistent clarity of purpose correlates with success. When you are unclear about what you want in your life, other people will happily design your life for you! Spend the time, have the conversations, hire a coach, do whatever it takes, but just get clear on how you want to use this one precious life.

How do you get clear? Pay attention to what you love, what you like to discuss. What occupies your daydreams? What do you read? Look for patterns and overlap. But most importantly, honor that still, small voice within.

You must also have skill and passion for your endeavor. I am in my mid-50s and good physical shape. I play basketball on the Massachusetts Senior Women's basketball team, the Mass Miracles. (Yes, it's a miracle we are still playing ball at our age!) I love basketball and am a decent player, yet it would not be a prudent desire for me to pursue a career as a player in the WNBA. The passion might be there, but the skill and "goodness of fit" is not.

Mitch Horowitz in his book *The Miracle of a Definite Chief Aim* writes "I believe true desires are realistic…An authentic desire is an achievable desire."

My friend, Craig, has been an aspiring actor and musician for the past 30 years. He has worked at Disney as a waiter to keep himself afloat financially. There are times when I wished he would give up on his dream so he could settle into a career and have a more comfortable life. But he persisted, working as a waiter, and applying for parts in movies, commercials, and plays. He would occasionally land jobs and published some music CDs. His desire and willingness to stay the course proved what Mitch Horowitz wrote: that an authentic desire is an achievable desire.

Now, in his mid 50s with salt-and-pepper hair, Craig has begun landing one acting job after another. His music is also gaining significant recognition on the Indie charts, and he is winning music awards. Craig was able to withstand his fear of failure and criticism of others in the pursuit of his dream. His desires are fulfilled, and he is happier than I have ever seen him. He is making money and living his dream.

So how do you know if your desire is authentic, or some egomaniacal fantasy? I believe if you meet these five criteria, then you have a genuine desire that requires your attention, love, willingness, and effort to bring forth. If you bring it forth, it will save you.

**1. You are willing to do the work**. For your desire to be birthed into existence, it will require focus, attention, time, effort, energy, and a huge commitment. I remember when my spouse and I decided to have children. For most married couples, that is a straightforward plan. For us, however, it involved numerous steps and decisions that ultimately ended up with the adoption of our son. The process spanned over four years, hundreds of hours of discussion and more meetings with various professionals than I can count. We had a commitment that took on a life of its own and gained momentum over the years. We were willing to do the work of becoming parents (and we remain delighted that we did!).

**2. You are ready to sacrifice**. Creating wealth — or anything else, for that matter — requires some level of sacrifice. David Ryback, Ph.D., in his book *Secrets of a Zen Millionaire*, talks about the necessary sacrifices one needs to make to get out of debt. If you are committed to creating a better financial future, you must be willing to make a few sacrifices along the way. David writes that debt is a modern social illness. If this is an "illness" that you suffer, you must be willing to do things differently – i.e., earn greater sums of money and spend more prudently – to create the financial future you desire.

**3. It lights you up**. Given that creating an expansive economic future requires effort, focus, and sacrifice, it is important that how you pursue wealth lights you up! Your passion and desire are something you find deeply gratifying and fulfilling – so much so that you would do it whether you get paid or not!

**4. You have genuine skill and enthusiasm about it.** I am passionate and enthusiastic about sports, but at my age and ability, there's no chance of my turning to a career as a professional athlete. To know if your desire is authentic and worthy of your time, energy, and effort, be sure that it is an area that comes naturally to you. You don't have to be the top performer – you can always acquire more skill over time – but you must possess some level of "natural talent."

I knew that I could likely succeed as a speaker after giving a talk in front of a large audience under the bright spotlights. I was so terrified on stage and that I could feel my butt muscles quivering! I had never spoken under lights before and didn't know in advance that I would not be able to see anyone in the audience while I was speaking. When I finished my piece, I stepped off the stage, certain I had just ruined my speaking career, when the man from the sound booth greeted me.

"I have been doing this work at conferences for almost 30 years," he said, "and I have never seen anyone deliver like you just did. That was incredible. You are such an authentic, natural speaker!"

I was flabbergasted. I laughed and said, "I guess that means you couldn't see my butt muscles quivering?" He laughed and assured me that I looked composed and connected to the audience.

You will know that your desire is authentic when you can excel even when you are up against your fears, uncertainties, and insecurities. Your natural skill and enthusiasm will carry you further than you might expect.

**5. You are willing to persist over time.** Like the story of my friend Craig, you must be prepared to endure over time for your desire to be manifest. Some come quickly, some more slowly, but when you take clear, prudent action, aligned with your desire, in the context of high vibe beliefs, you will experience success if you persist. Most people who are dubbed an "overnight success" laugh at the notion and are quick to say that they have been working at their craft for sometimes 10, 20 or even 30 years before becoming an "overnight success!"

What you desire desires expression through and as you. And when you fulfill a desire, new ones emerge. That is the natural order of human evolution. Learn to pay attention to and honor those persistent desires. The path and process of fulfilling them will lead you to a life of magic, wonder, and delight.

# CHAPTER 9

# Fulfilling Your Desire

*Desire: The starting point of all achievement.*
*— Napoleon Hill*

Your desires get fulfilled through creating a vision of what you want, breaking that vision into goals and then, as Tony Robbins says, taking massive action on your plans. The crux of this formula is that it is not as linear as it sounds. The odd irony is that once you start taking action, "Providence moves" in ways you could not have foreseen or predicted. Circumstances appear that support your path. The spark that ignites the flame is your clarity about what you want and your willingness to take action to bring it forth.

When I committed to being an empowerment speaker and teacher, I created a vision board to allow my imagination to expand with images of what I wanted to bring forth. One of my goals was to be a TED speaker – the mark of validation for speakers and thought leaders. I placed some TED images and TED speakers on my vision board and left it at that.

The next month, I got a Facebook message from a woman who previously filmed me speaking at an event. Her message said something like this: "Hi Jackie! I hope this finds you well. I wanted to let you know that I just received a TEDx license and am going to be producing a TEDx event in Massachusetts in two months. You were the first person I thought of when I got the permit. Would you be able to speak at it?"

Would I be able to speak at it? Of course! I did not fill out a bunch of TEDx applications. I did not ask anyone if they had connections to people creating a TED event. I did not contact the TED organization (all wise actions, mind you!). I simply put it on my vision board and continued about my business of speaking and teaching.

The process of fulfilling a desire is not always that fast. There are times when it takes years or even decades to see the outcome of your desire fulfilled. When you focus on your vibe, believing in your vision and taking aligned actions, things sometimes unfold very quickly.

To change your financial future, create a new vision of what is possible. Do you think you will be the having the same experience of money in the future as you are having now? If not, what do you imagine? See yourself as wiser, more centered, wealthier, and more successful. How does that look and feel? What does that bring into your life that you don't have now?

What I love about vision work is that it forces you to think about and focus on what you want. Napoleon Hill, the celebrated author of *Think and Grow Rich*, wrote that desire is the starting point of all achievement. "A BURNING DESIRE TO BE, AND TO DO is the starting point from which the dreamer must take off. Dreams are not born of indifference, laziness, or lack of ambition."

I have spent thousands of hours in conversations with people about their lives. What I see repeatedly is that people are very skilled at talking about what they *don't want* but show insufficient insight and commitment in talking about what they *do want*.

That is a fatal flaw in the quest for happiness and fulfillment. If you feel you don't know what you want (I hear that far too often as well), just think about what you persistently complain about or don't want in your life. You will only commit to doing the work of changing your Money Vibe if you have a burning desire for a different experience.

You would also be amazed to find that you can very likely have the essence of what you want money for right now. By "the essence of" something, I mean that you can probably find ways right now to achieve what you think money will provide you in the future. You do this by thinking and acting creatively and by changing your BEAT.

Suppose you want an extra $800 a month to hire a fitness trainer. What is the essence of that desire? The essence could be that you seek structure and accountability for a fitness routine, combined with proper knowledge. How can you receive the essence of that desire without spending the $800 a month, or whatever it is, to hire a trainer? You could get a workout buddy, commit to a time and place to meet for workouts, take fitness classes on YouTube (there are tons of excellent ones) and monitor your progress. You could take turns coming up with new, healthy recipes and cooking together after your workouts. The experience would likely deepen your friendship with that person and will give you the same result without the financial outlay.

The same principle applies to many of the things you desire. I remember once I was working with a coach and complaining that I wanted more time (hence the topic of my last book!). She asked me what I wanted the time for, what I would do with the time. I told her I just wanted to slow down, read more, and enjoy some relaxing time alone. She asked me why I had not done that already. I told her it was because I was too busy doing other things. She quickly pointed out that I was showing what I value by the choices of how I spend my time – and when I truly value reading and relaxing more, I would spend my time that way.

People use time and money as an excuse far too often. If you are committed to something – whether it is making more money or starting a business or having a child - you will find a way.

Creating your financial vision means spending time reflecting on what you want and why you want it: the thing or experience – and the essence as well. It is important that you remain open to receiving the essence of what you want rather than just the form.

My coaching client Becky wanted money so she could buy a home. When her sole focus was on the money, she kept feeling frustrated at how long the process was taking. I asked Becky to describe the essence of having her own home. She got quiet, and then with the most peaceful voice she said, "Having a home means stability, comfort, familiarity, and being able to care for it in any way I desire." The energy in her voice was palpable. I told her to spend the next several days and weeks focused on that essence – creating a home where she feels stability, comfort, familiarity, and the ability to care for it in any way she desired.

Within a month of her shifting focus, her mother asked her to move into her home as she was getting on in years and no longer wished to live alone. At first, Becky was reluctant to make such a commitment. Then she realized that such a move was the exact essence of what she had previously written down. She was astounded and soon accepted her mother's invitation.

What occurred over the coming years was beyond what Becky could have imagined. She and her mother repaired long-standing grievances with one another. They became good friends, and her mother became a primary support of Becky's career success. She had a better financial situation since her mother's home carried no mortgage. The home was in the exact location Becky wanted to live and, because she had extra money, she was able to create interior renovations to care for her home to her specific desires. That all occurred without her bringing more money into her life!

When you know what you want and believe it can be brought into your life, you are well on your way to having it. Your desired outcome must be in the realm of believability for you. No idea presented to the mind can be brought to fruition unless the mind accepts and believes it (hence, the importance of intentionally creating empowering beliefs). It is fine for it to be a stretch – beyond what you have created or experienced before – but still within what you believe is possible. Let me give you an example.

I teach an empowerment program called "Living a Transcendent Life." During one section we were studying how to bring forth your vision. By way of example, I initiated a project during the program where I committed to earning an additional $30,000 over the next 90 days. I saw that number as a stretch – it would be $10,000 a month beyond what I already had "in the books" with current contracts, classes, and clients. While it was a stretch, I also fully believed I could accomplish it with the right focus. I had no idea how, but I committed to the group that it would occur. What happened over the next two months was extraordinary. I tracked every cent of unexpected income and enthusiastically celebrated each time more arrived. A $14.95 rebate check from the phone company? That's great! Celebrate! A $150 repayment from our insurance company? Awesome! A new client signed up for a coaching package? Fabulous! That is how each day unfolded. I kept track of the inflow in the memo app on my phone, so each day I knew where I stood in relation to my goal.

I ended up with more work than I anticipated and created the extra $30,000 in 60 days, not 90! I was in the zone of the power of 4E formula of the energy of enthusiasm, excitement, and expectancy. It was exhilarating.

I decided I would "double my money" and say that I would earn another $30,000 in the month that was left in the program I was teaching. When I told the class, I could feel in my bones that it was "beyond my realm of believability" but I wanted to try it out. Nothing happened. No further income that I recall came my way at all. It was beyond my realm of believability.

I once read a card with a quote from Esther Hicks "If you do not yet have what you want, it is because you are not yet the vibratory match for your desire." I remember thinking, "That is such crap! There is no such thing as being a 'vibratory match' for your desire." That was before I started studying the power of your vibe!

In my experiment, I was a vibratory match for $30,000 in 60 days, but I was not a vibratory match for another $30,000 in 30 days!

# Creating Your Financial Vision

To create your financial vision, write a list of what you want (after doing some soul-searching to be sure it is really what you want and that you believe you can have it) and the time frame in which you desire it. I know you want everything "now," but bringing forth your desires is not the same as wishful thinking. "I wish I had…" does not have enough emotional energy to bring the conditions into your life. You simply make a list of what you desire financially. I strongly suggest you work with a three- to five-year timeline. Less than three years doesn't give sufficient time to develop momentum toward larger desires, and greater than five years gets too amorphous and vague. I find that a three- to five-year window gives you enough time to dig in while still being firmly in the realm of believability.

Your written vision would look something like this:

➢ By X date (three to five years in the future), I will:

- o Be free of all consumer debt.

- o Be earning $X a month through _____.

- o Be receiving money through multiple streams of income from these various sources: _____, _____ and _____.

- o Have paid down my mortgage to below $X.

- o Have $X in retirement funds.

- o Have created an educational fund for the children and have contributed $X

- o Have consistently given 10% of all earnings to _____ (contribution).

The method above is just an example to get you thinking about your financial vision. There is no "right vision." Your entire vision could be about giving to others or about how you want to feel regarding money. Social entrepreneur Taylor Conroy is someone whose vision is about giving and inspiring others. Taylor is the co-founder of WeJourney, a company that combines fundraising, philanthropic activity, and travel. WeJourney's goal is to scale the human emotion of empathy world-wide, and their method is to create viral fundraising campaigns via social media that lead to social impact projects in developing countries. WeJourney created thousands of projects and impacted hundreds of thousands of lives in a very short time. The positive impact began with a vision that occurred when Taylor decided to travel the world for a year and had his heart broken wide open by orphaned children in an African village decimated by AIDS.

This approach of creating a vision aligned with your values and carried inside of a high Money Vibe is not magical thinking. Your vision must have legs to it that will put the dynamic forces of the universe to work for you. What will you contribute in exchange for the inflow of money into your life? Get clear on what you want to receive and on how you will give. Napoleon Hill details a formula for turning your vision into a reality. His steps include:

1.  Determine what you want.

2.  Determine what you will give in return.

3.  Establish a definite date by which you will have your intended good.

4.  Create a definite plan for carrying out your desire.

5.  Write a clear, concise statement of what you desire, when you will achieve it, and by what means you will advance your desire.

6.  Read that statement aloud twice daily, feeling the energy of your desire fulfilled.

Notice that it all begins with knowing what you want – honoring your desire. When you establish your intention or goal in writing and say it aloud, "your frontal lobes can more efficiently direct your motor cortex to carry out your desire as you actively engage with others in the world. It's an extraordinary process: You begin with a goal-oriented thought, and the more you focus on it, the more your brain begins to plot out strategies to carry that thought into the world." (Newberg and Waldman, How God Changes Your Brain).

# Amp Up Your Vibe

Feeling your desire and the positive emotions of your desires fulfilled are critical components to elevating your vibe. How do you feel those emotions if you have yet to bring forth your desires? I think this is the coolest piece of this book. You can learn to create your desires so much faster using a neural process called creative imagination. The power of your imagination is your most underutilized superpower. In many ways, I believe the power of your creative imagination is even more important than your ability to create step-by-step plans and processes.

I believe that my TED talk experience was a direct result of this superpower. When I was creating the vision board and filling it with TED speakers and the TED logo, I was infusing my imagination with the feelings of being on the stage, under the lights, enjoying the energy of giving a powerful and successful talk. When I created $30,000 in 60 days, I would go to bed every night and imagine doing a happy dance with my family (one of my favorite things to do!) and giving high fives to celebrate the accomplishment. I felt the feelings I would have upon completion of the goal. It was all happening in my imagination. Engaging your imagination makes it easier for your brain to translate ideas into actions that bolster your goals.

At the exact time I got the last check in the mail that put me over the $30,000 mark, I was in the exact spot I had held in my mind, and my family was there with me in that exact moment. We danced, laughed, and gave each other high fives. It was great fun. But I had already had the experience in my mind. The longer you focus on your desires, the more real they feel.

The power of imagination does more than set your neural process in motion. As you engage others in your dream by sharing your vision, expressing your passion, and talking about your goals, they will feel your energy, enthusiasm, and excitement. Consequently, they have similar circuits that get stimulated, which sparks their motivation to assistance with your goals and dreams. You cannot accomplish what you desire in a vacuum.

Employing the power of creative imagination means that you create positive mental images, feelings and statements of your dream fulfilled. We spend so much time in mindless mental meandering. Be careful not to confuse the drone of mental chatter with thinking! It is not! It is simply the neurological firing that occurs in your brain. Thinking means establishing a fixed idea in your mind and then contemplating it.

Determine your vision and then create a mental image of the vision completed. Establish a few phrases that reflect your completed vision. Andrew Newberg and Mark Waldman write "the visualization process makes it easier for the brain to translate ideas into concrete attainable goals." (*How God Changes Your Brain*).

Here are some examples of mental images:

- Sitting on the porch of your new home.

- Seeing your new car sitting in your driveway.

- Standing on the stage with the audience smiling and applauding for you.

- Holding hands with your spouse on the beach after sending your last child off to college.

- Writing "paid in full" across your mortgage paperwork.

Notice that none of these mental images focus on how the dream was created.

The focus is on the *completion of the wish fulfilled* not simply on the attainment of money.

Here are some ideas for statements to enhance your Money Vibe:

- My financial life gets better every day.

- I have more than enough money to enjoy life and share with others.

- Money comes to me in unexpected ways for the good of all concerned.

- I have doubled my income by this time next year.

- My Money Vibe enhances all that I think, do and create.

- I am filled with joy as I celebrate increasing financial gains.

Repeat these statements as you drive to work, take a shower, wait in line at the grocery store or wait for a meeting to begin. Feel the positive vibe that these statements engender in you. How are you normally using your mind during those times? You are likely engaged in unproductive mind chatter or staring at your phone. Neither of those activities uses the incredible power of your brain to your advantage.

There is power and magic in creating your financial life with clarity and intention, aligned with your values and the vision for what you desire. There is no other path I have found that leads to such a rich, fulfilling, and rewarding life – a life where money flows with ease.

# Look at How Far You Have Come!

# Concluding Thoughts and Committed Actions

By now you realize that achieving financial freedom is as much an inside job as it is an income-generating strategy. It is not about having the perfect portfolio, but about having an elevated mindset and Money Vibe. Yes, there are things you need to do, but once you understand the inner workings of money as the flow (currency) of energy into and out of your life, you are well on your way to achieving the financial life you desire. You do not need money for what you have already been given: insight, awareness, consciousness, creativity, love, and life itself.

There is no one method or path to financial freedom. There is no simple, easy way to quiet the powerful hold that money has over our emotions and our lives. What will alter your experience is elevating your Money Vibe and, in doing so, realizing that what you desire also seeks expression through you. By listening to, honoring, and crafting your life after your desires, you are honoring the energy of life itself. What you desire is stronger than money. You want a deeper, more extraordinary experience of life itself. No amount of wealth will deliver that to you. You can have all the money in the world, but if you are imprisoned with a host of painful emotions or harboring a plethora of negative attitudes, you will never be truly free.

Where do you go from here? How do you leave this conversation and not get devoured with money situations once again? There is such tremendous pressure in our culture around outer productivity, doing, and earning rather than on self-development, joy, peace of mind and love. There is a feeling of constant hurry and chaos that invades our lives. Everything must be done fast! Cultivate the belief that you have all the time you need to fulfill your desires and your life purpose. Relax. Allow yourself to feel a sense of inner peace about money.

First and foremost, know that knowledge doesn't change anything! Only when you apply what you have learned will you create a new experience. Do the exercises in this book and work with your MVP to focus on elevating your Money Vibe.

Get clear on what you want by writing your vision based on your core financial values. Then use that clarity to consistently set small specific goals. Researchers Teresa Amabile and Steven Kramer found that the most important factor in maintaining success and motivation is everyday progress toward stated, meaningful goals. Most people start out with a flare and then fizzle out with nothing to show for it. That is what I call "metafizzle!" You get all excited about starting out on a new path, but without accountability, clarity, and making small, consistent progress, you will likely fizzle out on your hopes and dreams.

Don't ask, "Can I change my financial future?" Ask instead, "*How will* I change my financial future?" and then act on your ideas. When I was in graduate school, I got very creative to have enough money to get by – doing laboratory tests and paid clinical trials to help make ends meet. Many of you have probably done similar things. Here is the key:

It is the *same mental process* going from "What can I do to just get by?" to "What can I do to flourish financially?"

Determine now what you will focus on first. Write down three Committed Actions and *specifically when you will take them*. Then go to your calendar and schedule them!

Determine your committed actions:

_____

_____

_____

_____

Determine your affirmative statements:

_____

_____

_____

_____

Determine your new financial beliefs:

_____

_____

_____

_____

Commit these to memory and begin mentally repeating them whenever you are idle. Or if you want to have even more fun, turn your affirmations and beliefs into a jingle and sing them. I do that all the time before speaking engagements. Singing the phrases in a jingle works wonders for raising your vibe! You can't be grouchy walking around singing, "I am happy, healthy, wealthy, healed and whole" to the tune of "If You're Happy and You Know It!"

You should already have done the writing exercises in this book, but if you have not done so, start there. Work on your Financial Strong Foundation and your Financial Satisfaction Inventory. If you just increase your scores on those inventories while simultaneously elevating your vibe, I promise you that you will have a new experience of money in your life.

Once you begin shifting your vibe, you become a stronger, clearer, and better version of yourself. You like yourself more. Your heart will expand. You will want to earn more so you can give more. Neuroscience tells us via brain scans that giving to others activates motivation and reward centers of the brain. The more you earn, the more you can give, and the more you give, the more you are motivated to continue the giving process. It is a beautiful cycle! The more you do so, the more other people receive the benefits of your higher vibe. They see your success, they feel your peacefulness, and therein they feel hopeful.

Perhaps the most important reason to do the work of this book is to help alleviate the profound stress felt by most people in our culture regarding money. A rising tide lifts all boats. When you create inner peace through raising your vibe, you create energetic conditions that have a positive impact on others and serve as a model of someone who is financially free – whether you have lots of money or not. You can be the rising tide in your corner of the world. As George Bernard Shaw once wrote, "I would rather be a force of nature than a feverish clod of ailments and grievances complaining that the world will not devote itself to making me happy." Be that force of nature by dedicating your life to raising your vibe. The more people raise their vibe, the more the world heals. What would the world be like if everyone in the world raised their vibe? Wars would cease, hunger would end, and people would live with peace, love, and compassion.

Focus on your financial values when making financial decisions. Be sure that your financial vision includes giving to others, creating a legacy or some form of charitable giving. As you practice these steps, notice how you feel. You will sense your vibe elevating, your happiness expanding and your overall sense of freedom compounding.

Money can provide so many things in life. It is a tool and an energy source that allows for greater flow in so many ways. Consider it part of your spiritual journey to grow your Money Vibe. The more you do so, the more the world a better place for everyone. And isn't that what we are all seeking after all?

I am beyond excited that you have embarked on this journey with me. I cannot wait to hear what you create in your life because of changing your Money Vibe. I truly believe that by engaging in this work, you are entering the domain of miracles – where your dreams come true, and life unfolds with the same magical orchestration that has the universe operating with incredible perfection. I hope to have the joy of hearing your story. Use this book and my courses as a guide. Don't try to master all these principles alone. Devote yourself to elevating your vibe and your consciousness. Marry yourself to your compelling why. Limit all other distractions and let the life force that is orchestrating the galaxies and the universe work for and through you. This is my hope and prayer for you. You are worth it. Let's create a Vibe Tribe of people supporting one another toward true financial freedom!

Your vibe impacts the entire world. As every one of us elevates our vibe, all of humanity changes! Go light your world!

# Acknowledgements

No book is created without a committed, competent team supporting each step of the way. My profound appreciation and gratitude go to the following people who love and support me and helped me create this book. For each of you, I am eternally grateful: Aaron C. Yeagle, Amy Joslin, Rose Couzzo, Juliet LeBlanc, Cynthia Smith, June Damrow, Jo Welch, Kathy Kenyon, Noreen Daly-McArdle, Heidi Tran, Marcia Wieder, Doug Krueger, Gordon Tredgold, Bruce Schneider, Ralph Sanders, Valarie Eagan, Stephanie Roy; my Life Design, Life Mastery, and Living a Transcendent Life students; the wonderful members of the Vibe Tribe with Jackie Woodside on Facebook who weighed in on the title of the book and answered questions.

Most of all, I express my heart-felt gratitude to my son, Nathan Woodside, for tolerating your Mommy while she's writing a book! I know it's not easy being an author's kid! I love you endlessly.

# References

1. Altucher, James. *The Choose Yourself Guide to Wealth.* Choose Yourself Media, 2015.

2. Amabile, Teresa and Steven Kramer. *The Progress Principle: Using Small Wins to Ignite Joy, Engagement and Creativity at Work.* Harvard Business Review Press, 2011.

3. Bach, David. *The Automatic Millionaire Workbook: A Personalized Plan to Live and Finish Rich…Automatically.* Broadway Books, 2005.

4. De Neve, Jan-Emmanuel and Andrew Oswald. *Estimating the influence of life satisfaction and positive affect on later income using sibling fixed effects.* Proceedings of the National Academy of Sciences, vol. 109, no. 49, July 10, 2012.

5. Eker, T. Harv. *Secrets of the Millionaire Mind: Mastering the Inner Game of Wealth.* Harper Business, 2005.

6. Engelhart, Terces and Matthew. *Sacred Commerce: Business as a Path to Awakening.* North Atlantic Books, 2008.

7. Fisher, Mark. *The Millionaire's Path: Passion, Optimism and Wealth.* MJF Books, 1997.

8. Hill, Napoleon. *Think and Grow Rich: Official Publication of the Napoleon Hill Foundation,* 2016 (original publication 1937).

9. Horowitz, Mitch. *The Miracle of a Definite Chief Aim.* Gildan Press, 2017.

10. Kostigen, Thomas. Mind over money. Market Watch, June 27, 2002.

11. McKeown, Greg. *Essentialism: The Disciplined Pursuit of Less.* Crown Business, 2014.

12. Mosher, David and Skye Gould. How likely are foreign terrorists to kill Americans? The odds might surprise you. Business Insider, January 31, 2017.

13. National Endowment for Financial Education. (NEFE.org).

14. Needleman, Jacob. *Money and the Meaning of Life.* Currency Doubleday, 1991.

15. Newberg, Andrew, M.D., and Mark Robert Waldman. *How God Changes Your Brain: Breakthrough Findings from Leading Neuroscientists.* Ballantine Books, 2010.

16. Keller, Gary (with Jay Papasan). *The One Thing: The Surprisingly Simple Truth Behind Extraordinary Results.* Bard Press, 2012.

17. Kiyosaki, Robert. *Rich Dad, Poor Dad.* Warner Books, 1997.

18. Orman, Suze. *The 9 Steps to Financial Freedom: Practical and Spiritual Steps So You Can Stop Worrying,* Three Rivers Press, 2000.

19. Robbins, Tony. *Unshakeable: Your Financial Freedom Playbook, Creating Peace of Mind in a World of Volatility.* Simon and Schuster, 2017.

20. Ryback, David, Ph.D. *Secrets of a Zen Millionaire: 8 Steps to Personal Wealth with Real Estate, Living More Happily and*

*Getting Rich by Doing the Right Thing.* Motivational Press, 2015.

21. Seth, Anil. *Your Brain Hallucinates Your Conscious Reality.* TED.com, April 2017.

22. Success Magazine Staff, Special report: Introducing the You Economy, June 16, 2016. (http://www.success.com/article/introducing-the-youeconomy).

23. Sherman, Rachel. What the rich won't tell you. The *New York Times*, September 8, 2017.

24. Twenge, Jean. Have smartphones destroyed a generation? The Atlantic, September 2017.

# About the Author

Jackie Woodside is a TEDx speaker and has authored two best-selling books, "Calming the Chaos: A Soulful Guide to Managing Your Energy Rather than Your Time" and "Time for a Change: Essential Skills for Managing the Inevitable." Inc. Magazine selected her book "Calming the Chaos" as one of the Top Ten Motivational Books of 2015.

Jackie is the founder of the Curriculum for Conscious Living, a three-part empowerment program that helps people consistently live in a high vibe state. She also offers consulting, professional development training, keynote speeches, and spiritual retreats around the country. She has been a guest faculty member at the Unity Institute and has led leadership programs for Gallaudet University, the Massachusetts Executive Office of Health and Human Services, and many other institutions.

# Other Books by Jackie Woodside

*Calming the Chaos: A Soulful Guide to Managing Your Energy Rather than Your Time*

*Time for Change: Essential Skills for Managing the Inevitable*

## Connect with Jackie

www.JackieWoodside.com

www.MoneyVibeMethods.com

www.TheLifeDesignCourse.com

www.CalmingTheChaos-Book.com

Join The Vibe Tribe with Jackie Woodside on Facebook

Twitter @JackieWoodside

Connect via email at Jackie@JackieWoodside.com

Printed in Great Britain
by Amazon

80206293R00098